Develop High Quality Video Games with c++ and Unreal

Develop Cinematic, Interactive, and Hyper-Realistic Games Using Unreal Engine and C++ Mastery

SIMON TELLIER

Table of Contents

Chapter 1: Introduction to Unreal Engine and C++ Game Development

1.1 Why Unreal Engine and C++ Still Dominate

The game development world has evolved at a rapid pace, but when it comes to building visually striking, high-performance, and scalable games, Unreal Engine coupled with C++ remains the gold standard. From indie developers to top-tier AAA studios, Unreal Engine is used to build games that push boundaries across PC, console, and mobile platforms.

C++ continues to be the primary language for real-time, resource-critical applications. It offers unparalleled control over performance, memory management, and system-level programming—key areas in modern game development where every frame and every millisecond counts. While scripting languages like Python or Lua offer simplicity, they lack the deep integration, predictability, and efficiency that C++ provides when writing engine-level gameplay systems.

Unreal Engine enhances C++ with its own framework—reflection macros, memory management mechanisms, and actor component systems that are specifically tailored for games. Developers can build sophisticated mechanics, AI systems, physics simulations, and UI functionality that not only look good but perform exceptionally across diverse hardware profiles. This tight coupling between engine and language is what gives Unreal and C++ their enduring dominance.

1.2 Unreal vs. Unity vs. Custom Engines

Choosing a game engine often comes down to a balance between accessibility, performance, and control. Unity, for instance, is widely praised for its ease of use and rapid prototyping abilities, particularly for mobile and 2D games. Its C# scripting environment offers high-level functionality that's ideal for quick development cycles.

Unreal Engine, on the other hand, is engineered for those who need depth. Its default rendering capabilities are AAA-grade out of the box—features like Lumen global illumination, Nanite virtualized geometry, and physically-based material rendering require no extra setup. Unreal's level of visual fidelity and performance optimization is built-in, making it the go-to choice for studios aiming for cinematic experiences and photorealistic environments.

As for custom engines, they still have a place in projects that require extreme optimization or proprietary systems. However, they demand substantial time and specialized talent to maintain. What Unreal Engine offers is a compromise-free environment—cutting-edge rendering, deep customization with C++, and a development community that's vast and well-supported.

Unreal's ecosystem doesn't just compete—it leads in areas such as virtual production, VR/AR integration, and large-scale multiplayer architecture. When combined with the mastery of C++, Unreal becomes a platform not just for games, but for any real-time interactive experience imaginable.

1.3 What You'll Build in This Book

This book is designed around project-based learning, because nothing teaches better than building something real. Rather than isolated code examples or shallow tutorials, we will construct fully functional game systems and playable projects that mirror professional development pipelines.

You'll build three flagship projects throughout this book:

- **A third-person action-adventure game**, featuring character controllers, combat mechanics, camera systems, and environment interaction.

- **A cinematic walking simulator**, showcasing environmental storytelling, cutscene systems, and dynamic audio-visual triggers.

- **A lightweight multiplayer arena shooter**, where you'll learn about server-client architecture, replication, and session management.

These games are chosen not for novelty, but for the diversity of skills they teach. Each one focuses on different pillars of Unreal Engine mastery—single-player mechanics, narrative and cinematic systems, online networking, and scalable C++ architecture. The final result will not only be three portfolio-ready games but a full understanding of how to build and scale Unreal Engine projects for real-world deployment.

1.4 Development Environment Setup: UE5, Visual Studio, Git

Before writing your first line of code, a well-configured environment is critical. Unreal Engine works best when paired with Visual Studio, Git, and a few essential tools. Here's how to set it up:

1. **Install the Epic Games Launcher.** Through it, you can download the latest version of Unreal Engine 5. Make sure to install any sample content you might want to experiment with later.

2. **Install Visual Studio (2022 or later).** During installation, select the "Desktop Development with C++" workload. Ensure you also include the Windows SDK,

MSVC toolset, and CMake tools. Unreal uses these to compile, link, and debug C++ projects.

3. **Configure Git for version control.** Unreal Engine projects can grow to include thousands of files. Use Git to track your changes, protect your progress, and collaborate if you're working with others. Install Git LFS (Large File Storage) to handle binary assets like .uasset and .umap files.

4. **Optional tools**:

   ○ **GitHub Desktop** for a GUI-based Git experience

   ○ **Visual Assist or ReSharper C++** to enhance code navigation in Visual Studio

   ○ **Epic Games' Datasmith and Quixel Bridge** for importing high-fidelity assets

Once installed, make sure Unreal is correctly detecting Visual Studio. Open the engine and verify the compiler paths in the settings. A proper connection ensures that project files are generated with the necessary .sln solution files and include the correct targets for building and launching directly from your IDE.

1.5 Navigating the Unreal Editor

The Unreal Editor can initially feel overwhelming due to its size and richness. But once you understand its core layout, you'll find it remarkably efficient.

Here are the main panels and what they do:

- **Viewport**: Your window into the world. It shows your active scene and lets you position objects, preview lighting, and simulate gameplay.

- **World Outliner**: A hierarchical list of all objects in your current level. This includes actors, lights, cameras, and volume triggers.

- **Details Panel**: Displays properties and settings for any selected object. From transform values to component-specific options, this is where most editing happens.

- **Content Browser**: The hub for all project assets. It includes folders for meshes, textures, materials, blueprints, and C++ classes.

- **Toolbar**: Offers compile, build, play, and launch options, along with access to project settings, build configurations, and the Blueprint editor.

Navigating the editor quickly is key. Learn shortcuts like **F** to focus on a selected actor, **Alt + drag** to duplicate, and **G** to toggle Game View (which hides editor overlays). Customize your layout and save it if you're working across multiple monitors.

Familiarize yourself with **Play Modes**: in-editor play (PIE), standalone mode, and new window mode. Each serves different purposes—PIE is great for fast iteration, while standalone mode more accurately simulates packaged game behavior.

Unreal's UI is deeply integrated with its reflection system, so changes in C++ often propagate into the editor automatically if you use macros like UPROPERTY and UFUNCTION. This real-time feedback loop is a huge advantage over engines that separate code from the editor experience.

1.6 Unreal Project Structure and File Types

A typical Unreal project is composed of multiple directories and file types that are tightly integrated into the engine's build system and editor.

Here's a breakdown of the most critical components:

- **.uproject File**: The root of your project. This JSON-based file contains metadata about the project version, modules, and plugin configurations. It's what Unreal Engine reads to open your game.

- **Source Folder**: Contains all your C++ code, organized by modules. Each module is compiled independently and usually starts with a GameModule.cpp and GameModule.h file. You'll find your classes here—characters, game modes, components, UI logic.

- **Content Folder**: All non-code assets live here—textures, materials, blueprints, animations, particle effects. Unreal converts these into .uasset files, which are not human-readable but efficiently indexed.

- **Intermediate and Saved Folders**: Used for temporary and cached files like builds, logs, or shader compilation data. These folders can often be deleted when troubleshooting issues.

- **Build and Config Folders**: Contain build scripts, platform-specific settings, and initialization parameters like input mappings, default maps, and rendering targets.

As your project grows, maintaining a clean directory structure becomes essential. Organize your assets with naming conventions (SM_, BP_, M_ for static meshes, blueprints, and materials respectively). This not only improves readability but also helps with search, filtering, and debugging.

Understanding how Unreal links assets, compiles code, and loads scenes will save you hours of trial and error. You'll know exactly where to place new code, how to expose it to the editor, and how to keep things organized as your game scales in complexity.

This concludes Chapter 1, where you've now laid the groundwork for everything to follow. You understand why Unreal and C++ remain unmatched in the world of interactive 3D experiences, how they compare to alternatives, what projects you'll build, and how to prepare your environment for real development work.

Chapter 2: Mastering C++ for Unreal

2.1 C++ Essentials Tailored to Unreal Engine

C++ is a powerful but notoriously complex language, and when used within Unreal Engine, it behaves quite differently from conventional C++ programming. Unreal doesn't just use C++—it extends it through a custom build tool, reflection macros, memory management systems, and a gameplay framework. This is not general-purpose C++; it's C++ reimagined for building dynamic, high-performance games.

To begin working effectively in Unreal, you must understand how standard C++ maps to Unreal's conventions. For example, standard practices like using std::vector or std::string are replaced with Unreal's TArray and FString. These types are more than syntactic replacements—they integrate with the engine's reflection and garbage collection systems, making them safer and more performant within the engine context.

The Unreal Build Tool (UBT) compiles your code using predefined modules. Instead of a traditional main() function, your entry point is declared via IMPLEMENT_PRIMARY_GAME_MODULE, which tells Unreal how to start your game module and where your game's root logic lives.

The engine also favors the use of prefixes to denote types:

- A for Actor classes (APlayerCharacter)

- U for UObject-derived classes (UInventoryComponent)

- F for structs (FVector, FTransform)

- T for templates (TArray, TMap)

These prefixes aren't arbitrary—they reflect how each type participates in the Unreal object system. For instance, only UObject-derived classes participate in serialization, reflection, and garbage collection. Understanding this taxonomy is crucial for building clean, scalable systems.

2.2 Classes, Inheritance, and Smart Pointers in UE

Unreal Engine is deeply object-oriented, and inheritance forms the backbone of most gameplay programming. A typical Actor-based hierarchy might look like this:

- AActor → APawn → ACharacter → AMyCustomCharacter

Each level of this hierarchy adds new functionality. AActor provides location and transformation; APawn adds input and control; ACharacter introduces skeletal meshes and movement logic. When creating your own classes, you almost always derive from an existing engine base class to leverage built-in behaviors.

Unreal promotes composition through components, encouraging developers to break down functionality into reusable parts. For example, a UCameraComponent or UAudioComponent can be attached to an actor to grant it camera or audio capabilities without modifying the core class logic.

While raw pointers (*) and references (&) still exist, Unreal relies heavily on smart pointers to manage memory and ownership. The key types are:

- TWeakObjectPtr<> — A non-owning reference to an object.

- TSharedPtr<> and TSharedRef<> — Used outside of the UObject system for shared ownership.

- TUniquePtr<> — For exclusive ownership.

- UPROPERTY() pointers — Used to expose member variables to the garbage collector.

It's important not to use new and delete for UObjects—Unreal manages their lifecycle through its memory system. Use NewObject<> or CreateDefaultSubobject<> to instantiate UObjects or components, and let Unreal handle destruction automatically.

Inheritance in Unreal is designed with gameplay architecture in mind. You'll often override methods like BeginPlay(), Tick(), and SetupPlayerInputComponent() to customize behavior without reinventing the wheel. Combine this with clear pointer ownership semantics, and you have a foundation that's both powerful and safe.

2.3 Understanding the UCLASS, UPROPERTY, UFUNCTION Macros

At the heart of Unreal's extensible C++ model is its reflection system—a meta-programming system that allows C++ classes, variables, and functions to be recognized and used by the engine. This is made possible through macros like UCLASS, USTRUCT, UENUM, UPROPERTY, and UFUNCTION.

These macros aren't optional—they're what allow your C++ code to appear in the editor, be serialized, replicated, or manipulated through Blueprints.

- UCLASS() must be placed before any class you want Unreal to recognize. Without it, the class exists in C++, but not in the engine's eyes.

- UPROPERTY() tells the engine to track a variable. You can use specifiers like EditAnywhere, BlueprintReadWrite, VisibleDefaultsOnly, or Replicated to control how and where it appears.

- UFUNCTION() is used to expose C++ methods to Blueprints or enable networking features like remote procedure calls.

Here's a simple example of a class declaration that uses these macros effectively:

cpp

CopyEdit

```cpp
UCLASS()
class AMyCharacter : public ACharacter
{
    GENERATED_BODY()

public:
    AMyCharacter();

    UPROPERTY(EditAnywhere, BlueprintReadWrite, Category="Stats")
    float Health;

    UFUNCTION(BlueprintCallable, Category="Combat")
    void Attack();
```

};

These macros are parsed by Unreal Header Tool (UHT) before compilation. The engine then generates code behind the scenes to enable editor visibility, network replication, and garbage collection tracking.

Knowing how and when to use these macros isn't just about making your variables appear in the editor—it's about working harmoniously with the engine. Misusing or omitting them often results in undefined behavior or silent failures.

2.4 Working with UObject and Actor Lifecycle

Every object in Unreal that you want to serialize, expose to Blueprints, or include in gameplay should inherit from UObject. For anything that needs to exist in the world, you should inherit from AActor, which itself extends UObject and includes spatial properties.

UObjects are not placed in the world—they exist purely as logic containers, managers, or data holders. Things like inventory systems, weapon definitions, or UI data models often extend UObject.

Actors, on the other hand, are entities that exist in a level or scene. They are created dynamically or placed manually. Their lifecycle includes several important methods:

- Constructor — Initializes default values.

- PostInitializeComponents() — Called once all subobjects are created.

- BeginPlay() — Called when the actor is spawned or the level starts.

- Tick(float DeltaTime) — Called every frame if ticking is enabled.

- EndPlay() — Called when the actor is removed from the world.

Managing state transitions correctly is critical. Don't try to access other actors or components in the constructor—they might not be initialized yet. Instead, use BeginPlay() or OnComponentBeginOverlap() where appropriate.

Spawning actors is handled with GetWorld()->SpawnActor<>(), while destroying them uses Destroy(). Always use IsValid() or IsPendingKill() to check object validity before accessing them, especially in multiplayer or async scenarios.

2.5 Memory Management and Garbage Collection in UE

Manual memory management is one of the hardest parts of native C++ programming. Unreal simplifies this through an internal garbage collector for UObjects. However, there are still best practices and rules you need to follow.

Any UObject-derived class can be garbage collected, but only if it's not referenced by any other active object. To ensure persistence, member variables should be marked with UPROPERTY(); this flags them as referenced and prevents collection.

Here's what to avoid:

- Storing raw pointers to UObjects without UPROPERTY

- Using C++ arrays instead of TArray

- Creating UObjects with new or delete directly

Garbage collection runs periodically and checks for unreachable objects. If an object is no longer referenced by any valid UPROPERTY chain, it is marked for cleanup. That means your UObjects must be registered properly, even in temporary or dynamic contexts.

For non-UObject types, like FVector, FString, or user-defined structs, traditional memory rules apply. Use TUniquePtr or TSharedPtr if you're managing heap-allocated memory outside the UObject system.

You can trigger manual garbage collection with:

cpp

CopyEdit

```
GEngine->ForceGarbageCollection(true);
```

This is useful in memory-critical environments, such as mobile games or runtime-level streaming scenarios.

2.6 Practical C++ Patterns for Game Dev

Unreal Engine favors a modular, data-driven design. Here are some essential patterns you'll use repeatedly:

- **Component-Based Architecture**: Instead of monolithic inheritance trees, create reusable components. For example, a UHealthComponent can be attached to any actor, giving it health and damage logic.

- **Event Delegates**: Unreal uses its own delegate system for event broadcasting. DECLARE_DYNAMIC_MULTICAST_DELEGATE allows you to create custom events that can be bound in both C++ and Blueprints.

- **Singletons and Subsystems**: Use UGameInstance, UWorldSubsystem, and UGameplayStatics for managing global states or utility functions. This avoids static abuse and ensures testability.

- **Interfaces**: Unreal interfaces (UINTERFACE) allow for behavior contracts without inheritance. You can define interaction rules, AI commands, or ability behaviors that apply to multiple actor types.

- **Factories and Spawners**: Use SpawnActor patterns alongside data tables and factories to dynamically create game entities. This makes your game data-driven and designer-friendly.

- **Data-Only Blueprints**: Create C++ base classes with logic, and extend them into Blueprint subclasses with variables only. This separation lets designers tweak content without modifying code.

With these patterns, you'll be able to build gameplay systems that are robust, reusable, and performance-friendly—essential qualities for both solo developers and full teams working at scale.

Chapter 2 concludes your foundational education in Unreal's C++ model. You've now seen how the language is adapted to the engine's systems, how to use Unreal's macro-based reflection, and how to structure classes, memory, and patterns for maximum efficiency and clarity.

Chapter 3: Understanding the Gameplay Framework

3.1 GameMode, GameState, PlayerController, Pawn, and HUD

At the core of every Unreal Engine game lies its **Gameplay Framework**—a system of interrelated classes that define how the game runs, how players interact with the world, and how game rules are enforced. Understanding the roles of the five key classes—GameMode, GameState, PlayerController, Pawn, and HUD—is essential for designing coherent and functional game logic.

- **GameMode**: This is the rulebook. The AGameModeBase (or AGameMode) class dictates what happens when the game starts, how players spawn, how the game ends, and how scoring works. It's only relevant on the server side in multiplayer games, meaning it has no effect on clients.

- **GameState**: While GameMode governs logic, AGameStateBase exists to **replicate shared information to all clients**. It tracks global variables like match time, player teams, and scores—essential in multiplayer sessions for consistency.

- **PlayerController**: Every player is assigned a APlayerController when they join the game. This class acts as the input interpreter and bridge between the player and the world. It translates input into movement or actions and controls the player's Pawn.

- **Pawn**: The in-game representation of a player or AI agent. This can be a vehicle, character, or creature. If the Pawn is also a ACharacter, it inherits functionality like skeletal mesh animation and navigation.

- **HUD**: Heads-Up Display (HUD) is responsible for rendering on-screen elements. This might be done with legacy HUD classes using Canvas drawing, or through modern UI systems like UMG.

These classes work together to enforce clean separation of concerns. The GameMode dictates logic, the GameState synchronizes it, the PlayerController handles input, the Pawn embodies the player, and the HUD shows what matters on screen. You don't need all of them for every project, but ignoring their relationships will result in spaghetti code and hard-to-maintain systems.

3.2 The Game Loop: Ticks, Timers, and Delegates

Every real-time game relies on a **game loop**—a recurring cycle that updates input, logic, and rendering each frame. Unreal manages this loop behind the scenes, but gives developers multiple ways to hook into it.

- **Tick**: Classes that derive from AActor or UActorComponent can override Tick(float DeltaTime). This method is called once per frame if PrimaryActorTick.bCanEverTick is true. Use it sparingly—it's best for continuously updated logic like movement or state checks.

- **Timers**: Unreal's timer manager allows you to schedule functions to run after a delay or at intervals. This is more efficient than ticking when updates are not needed every frame:

cpp

CopyEdit

```
GetWorldTimerManager().SetTimer(MyHandle, this, &AMyActor::MyFunction, 2.0f,
true);
```

Timers are ideal for things like cooldowns, periodic damage, or AI decision updates.

- **Delegates**: Unreal's event system allows for decoupled communication between classes. You can bind and broadcast functions using delegates:

cpp

CopyEdit

```
DECLARE_DYNAMIC_MULTICAST_DELEGATE(FOnHealthDepleted);

FOnHealthDepleted OnHealthDepleted;


OnHealthDepleted.Broadcast();
```

This allows one class to notify others when something happens, without tightly coupling the two.

A good rule of thumb is to use **Tick for frame-specific updates**, **Timers for periodic logic**, and **Delegates for event-based communication**. Together, these systems give you full control over how your game responds to time and input.

18

3.3 Handling Inputs via Enhanced Input System

Input in Unreal Engine 5 is handled by the **Enhanced Input System**, which replaces the older input model with a more flexible and scalable architecture. It allows you to define **Input Actions**, **Input Mappings**, and **Contexts**, making input reusable and context-aware.

Instead of hardcoding keys or buttons, you define UInputAction assets and assign them to actions like "Jump" or "Fire." These are then bound in code:

cpp

CopyEdit

```
PlayerInputComponent->BindAction(MoveAction, ETriggerEvent::Triggered, this,
&AMyCharacter::Move);
```

The **Input Mapping Context** allows for layering different control schemes—for example, switching input layouts when opening a menu or changing control modes when entering a vehicle.

To set up Enhanced Input in C++:

1. Add the EnhancedInput plugin and module.

2. Create input action assets in the editor.

3. Add them to the player's input mapping context.

4. Bind the actions in SetupPlayerInputComponent().

19

This system supports:

- Gamepad, mouse, keyboard, and touch simultaneously

- Contextual remapping (menu vs. gameplay)

- Multiple bindings per action (e.g., both W and Up Arrow for movement)

The Enhanced Input System is especially useful in scalable games where player interaction changes across game states or different characters.

3.4 Actor Components vs. Inheritance

Game logic in Unreal can be composed through **inheritance** or **composition via components**. While both are valid, understanding when to use which is critical for clean architecture.

- **Inheritance**: Use it when you're extending core engine classes or designing variations of a base actor. For example, creating AEnemyGoblin, AEnemyTroll, and AEnemyDragon from a common AEnemyBase makes sense when they share core functionality and override specific behavior.

- **Actor Components**: Use them when you want to **add behavior modularly**. For example, a UHealthComponent or USaveComponent can be attached to any actor that needs that functionality, without changing the actor's class hierarchy.

Benefits of components:

- Reusability: One component works across many actors.

- Separation of concerns: Each component handles a single responsibility.

- Better testing: You can test components independently.

- Editor configurability: Designers can mix and match behaviors visually.

A typical example:

cpp

CopyEdit

```cpp
UHealthComponent* Health =
CreateDefaultSubobject<UHealthComponent>(TEXT("HealthComponent"));
```

Modern Unreal development favors composition. You might still use inheritance to set up a base gameplay class structure, but attach gameplay logic via components. This ensures flexibility and maintainability, especially in complex projects.

3.5 Creating Custom Player Character with C++

Creating a player character from scratch in C++ involves several steps that tie together input, movement, camera control, and component setup. A typical setup looks like this:

1. **Inherit from ACharacter**, which includes a CharacterMovementComponent.

2. **Add a SpringArm and Camera** for third-person or first-person perspectives.

3. **Setup input bindings** in SetupPlayerInputComponent().

4. **Implement movement logic** (walking, sprinting, jumping).

cpp

CopyEdit

```
AMyPlayerCharacter::AMyPlayerCharacter()
{
    SpringArm =
CreateDefaultSubobject<USpringArmComponent>(TEXT("SpringArm"));
    SpringArm->SetupAttachment(RootComponent);


    Camera = CreateDefaultSubobject<UCameraComponent>(TEXT("Camera"));
    Camera->SetupAttachment(SpringArm);
}
```

Use the movement component to control speed, jump height, and air control. For advanced control, override Tick() to respond to player states, and create custom input responses such as dashing, crouching, or climbing.

You'll also want to expose variables like MaxHealth, Stamina, and CurrentSpeed using UPROPERTY() so they can be modified via Blueprints or data assets. This allows for easy tuning without recompilation.

Integrating animation requires working with **Animation Blueprints**, which can receive values from your C++ character via AnimInstance subclasses and UFUNCTION bindings.

3.6 Blueprint vs. C++: Integration and Best Use Cases

Unreal Engine is unique in that it offers two development languages side-by-side: **C++** and **Blueprints**. Rather than choosing one over the other, the real power lies in **hybrid development**.

Use **C++ for**:

- Core gameplay systems (movement, health, combat)

- Performance-critical logic (AI, physics)

- Engine extensions (custom components, plugins)

- Version-controlled features (since Blueprints can be binary)

Use **Blueprints for**:

- Rapid iteration and prototyping

- Visual scripting for non-programmers

- Level scripting and event triggers

- UI logic and animations

Best practice: write a **C++ base class** with logic and expose key variables and functions using UPROPERTY and UFUNCTION. Then, create **Blueprint subclasses** for designers to work with.

For example:

cpp

CopyEdit

```cpp
UCLASS(Blueprintable)

class AEnemyBase : public ACharacter

{

    GENERATED_BODY()


public:

    UFUNCTION(BlueprintImplementableEvent)

    void OnDeath();

};
```

This setup allows C++ to handle engine logic, while designers can visually script what happens when an enemy dies—like playing an explosion or triggering a dialogue.

This separation encourages **clean architecture**: code stays deterministic and fast, while gameplay feel and polish remain in the designer's hands.

With Chapter 3 complete, you now understand how Unreal's gameplay framework is architected—from how the core classes interact, to how input, ticking, and game logic are composed. You've also built a working mental model for when to use Blueprints vs. C++, and how to architect game systems that scale with your project.

Chapter 4: Building a Third-Person Adventure Game (Project 1)

4.1 Designing the Core Mechanics

Before diving into code, every game needs a clear design blueprint. The third-person adventure game we're about to build will serve as your foundational project—a fully playable experience demonstrating movement, interaction, UI elements, and animation. The goal here isn't to overwhelm you with complexity, but to show how cohesive game systems are constructed from modular parts.

The core mechanics we'll implement include:

- **Character control** (walk, sprint, jump)

- **Perspective camera system**

- **Basic interaction logic** (open doors, activate switches)

- **Collectible system** (track and display items)

- **Animation sync** (character movement and idle states)

- **Gameplay loop trigger** (win condition when all collectibles are found)

These systems combine core pillars of Unreal's gameplay architecture: pawn movement, player input, animation logic, UI updates, and world interaction. Each piece teaches not just how to write code, but how to structure your logic so it's readable, reusable, and scalable.

Before you code, it's worth sketching out a rough layout of your level in the editor. Place basic geometry, define a start point, and set locations for interactions or collectibles. Even a grey-boxed map gives you a mental model for how the systems you're about to implement will come together in gameplay.

4.2 Importing Characters and Animations

Unreal Engine provides sample content, including the **Third Person Template**, which includes a rigged character mesh, animations, and a ready-to-use skeleton. We'll build from that to save time while focusing on game logic.

To begin:

1. **Create a new project** using the Third Person template.

2. Navigate to the Content/Character folder, and note the following key assets:

   - **SK_Mannequin** (skeletal mesh)

   - **ABP_Manny** (animation blueprint)

   - **Idle, Walk, Run, Jump animations**

   - **ThirdPerson_AnimBP** (the pre-made animation blueprint we'll enhance)

In your C++ project, create a new class that inherits from ACharacter, and set it up to use the mannequin mesh and animation blueprint. Here's a sample constructor setup:

cpp

CopyEdit

```
APlayerCharacter::APlayerCharacter()
{
    GetMesh()->SetSkeletalMesh(SomeSkeletalMesh);
    GetMesh()->SetAnimInstanceClass(UThirdPerson_AnimBP::StaticClass());
    GetMesh()->SetupAttachment(RootComponent);
}
```

Ensure the mesh is correctly rotated and positioned. Unreal characters face forward along the **X-axis**, so you may need to adjust the mesh rotation using SetRelativeRotation(FRotator(0.f, -90.f, 0.f)).

Using these base assets saves considerable animation setup time, allowing you to focus on gameplay systems. You can always swap in custom meshes or animations later once your systems are stable.

4.3 Implementing Movement, Jumping, and Sprinting

Now that we've linked a skeletal mesh to our C++ class, it's time to handle movement. Unreal's ACharacter class already includes a **CharacterMovementComponent**, which supports walking, jumping, and gravity by default. All we need to do is map inputs to actions.

In your character's SetupPlayerInputComponent function, bind the Enhanced Input actions for movement and jumping:

28

cpp

CopyEdit

void APlayerCharacter::SetupPlayerInputComponent(UInputComponent*
PlayerInputComponent)

{

    Super::SetupPlayerInputComponent(PlayerInputComponent);

    PlayerInputComponent->BindAxis("MoveForward", this,
&APlayerCharacter::MoveForward);

    PlayerInputComponent->BindAxis("MoveRight", this,
&APlayerCharacter::MoveRight);

    PlayerInputComponent->BindAction("Jump", IE_Pressed, this, &ACharacter::Jump);

    PlayerInputComponent->BindAction("Jump", IE_Released, this,
&ACharacter::StopJumping);

}

Define movement handlers that consider controller rotation:

cpp

CopyEdit

void APlayerCharacter::MoveForward(float Value)

{

29

```cpp
if (Controller && Value != 0.0f)
{
    const FRotator Rotation = Controller->GetControlRotation();

    const FVector Direction = FRotationMatrix(Rotation).GetUnitAxis(EAxis::X);

    AddMovementInput(Direction, Value);
}
}
```

For sprinting, create a boolean bIsSprinting flag, and adjust MaxWalkSpeed in BeginSprint() and EndSprint() functions. Use CharacterMovement->MaxWalkSpeed to change the speed dynamically.

This simple yet robust movement system gives you fluid third-person navigation with support for walking, sprinting, and jumping, all under C++ control.

4.4 Creating Camera Systems and Perspective Switching

The third-person camera system is built using a **Spring Arm Component** and a **Camera Component**. The spring arm smooths camera movement and allows for lag and rotation settings.

In the constructor of your player character:

cpp

CopyEdit

```cpp
SpringArm =
CreateDefaultSubobject<USpringArmComponent>(TEXT("SpringArm"));

SpringArm->SetupAttachment(RootComponent);

SpringArm->TargetArmLength = 300.f;

SpringArm->bUsePawnControlRotation = true;


Camera = CreateDefaultSubobject<UCameraComponent>(TEXT("Camera"));

Camera->SetupAttachment(SpringArm);

Camera->bUsePawnControlRotation = false;
```

To add **camera rotation**, bind inputs to AddControllerYawInput() and AddControllerPitchInput() in your input setup.

You can extend this to include **first-person switching** by adding a second camera component, storing both references, and enabling/disabling them with a keypress:

cpp

CopyEdit

```cpp
void APlayerCharacter::ToggleCameraPerspective()

{

    bIsThirdPerson = !bIsThirdPerson;

    ThirdPersonCamera->SetActive(bIsThirdPerson);
```

```
FirstPersonCamera->SetActive(!bIsThirdPerson);

}
```

This adds immersive perspective switching—useful for zoom mechanics, close combat, or player choice customization.

4.5 Using AnimBlueprints with C++

Animation in Unreal is driven by **Animation Blueprints**, which update based on movement and state parameters. These parameters are passed from your character class to the Animation Blueprint using the character's AnimInstance.

Create a custom AnimInstance subclass and add relevant variables like Speed, bIsInAir, or bIsSprinting.

From your character class:

cpp

CopyEdit

```
UCustomAnimInstance* AnimInstance =
Cast<UCustomAnimInstance>(GetMesh()->GetAnimInstance());

if (AnimInstance)

{

    AnimInstance->bIsSprinting = bIsSprinting;

}
```

In the Animation Blueprint's Event Graph, read these variables and feed them into a State Machine. The state machine will use transitions (e.g., Speed > 0) to move between idle, walking, running, and jumping states.

This separation allows you to handle all gameplay logic in C++ while allowing your designers to polish the feel of movement and responsiveness visually in Blueprints.

4.6 Adding Interactions, Collectibles, and Triggers

A game world isn't engaging without interactive elements. Let's implement a basic **interaction system** where players press a key to trigger an effect—open a door, activate a lever, or collect an item.

Start by defining a UInterface called IInteractable, which any interactive object can implement:

cpp

CopyEdit

```
UINTERFACE(BlueprintType)

class UInteractable : public UInterface

{

    GENERATED_BODY()

};


class IInteractable
```

```
{

    GENERATED_BODY()


public:

    UFUNCTION(BlueprintNativeEvent)

    void Interact();

};
```

In your player character, trace a short line in front of the player when the interaction key is pressed. If the hit actor implements IInteractable, call its Interact() method.

cpp

CopyEdit

```
FHitResult Hit;

FVector Start = Camera->GetComponentLocation();

FVector End = Start + (Camera->GetForwardVector() * 200.f);


FCollisionQueryParams Params;

Params.AddIgnoredActor(this);
```

```
if (GetWorld()->LineTraceSingleByChannel(Hit, Start, End, ECC_Visibility, Params))

{

   if (AActor* HitActor = Hit.GetActor())

   {

      if (HitActor->GetClass()->ImplementsInterface(UInteractable::StaticClass()))

      {

         IInteractable::Execute_Interact(HitActor);

      }

   }

}
```

For collectibles, create an ACollectibleItem actor with a collision sphere and a visual mesh. In its Interact() method, increase the player's score, destroy the item, and update a UMG widget showing collectible count.

Triggers can be implemented using Box Trigger volumes. When the player overlaps, you can display prompts, play sounds, or begin scripted events.

This final step brings life to your world—moving it from an environment to a reactive, goal-driven experience.

With Chapter 4 complete, you've built the foundation of a third-person adventure game. You've imported characters and animations, implemented responsive movement and camera control, and added interactive elements to drive gameplay. This isn't a toy demo—it's a playable, extensible system that can evolve into a real title.

Chapter 5: Advanced World Building and Visual Fidelity

5.1 Working with Landscapes and Foliage

A compelling game world begins with believable terrain. Unreal Engine's **Landscape system** offers procedural and sculptable environments at scale. It allows developers to shape hills, valleys, cliffs, and rivers with intuitive tools—ideal for adventure games that demand exploration across diverse topographies.

Start by creating a new **Landscape Actor** in your level:

- Use the **Landscape tool** from the Modes panel.

- Set resolution and section sizes based on gameplay scope (e.g., 63x63 components for a medium world).

- Sculpt using brushes—flatten, smooth, noise—to define elevations.

To texture the terrain, apply a **Landscape Material** using **Layer Blends**. Each layer corresponds to terrain types—grass, dirt, stone, etc. Use weight-blended layers to allow smooth transitions between them. This is ideal for games that visually communicate where players can travel or explore.

Foliage brings the world to life. Unreal's **Foliage Tool** lets you paint static meshes—grass, trees, rocks—directly onto terrain. For performance:

- Enable **Instanced Static Meshes (ISM)** for rendering efficiency.

- Use LODs to simplify distant visuals.

- Enable **Cull Distance Volume** to reduce draw calls.

For more control, procedurally generate foliage using **Blueprint Spawners** or **C++ logic**. You can apply placement rules—like "only spawn grass on slope under 15°" or "no trees within X units of player spawn."

Creating a landscape isn't about randomness. It's about establishing **visual rhythm** and **navigational clarity**—the subtle cues that invite players to explore or signal danger nearby.

5.2 Lighting Systems: Directional, Skylight, and Lumen

Lighting does more than illuminate; it defines **mood, time, atmosphere, and player focus**. Unreal Engine 5's **Lumen Global Illumination** system introduces dynamic lighting that reacts naturally to changes in environment, geometry, and camera angle—without baking lightmaps.

Your primary lights:

- **Directional Light**: Represents sun/moon. Set to **Moveable** for real-time dynamic shadows.

- **Sky Light**: Adds ambient light from the sky dome. Essential for outdoor scenes.

- **Sky Atmosphere + Volumetric Clouds**: Used together, they simulate realistic sky color transitions and volumetric clouds.

Tips for powerful lighting:

- Adjust **Indirect Lighting Intensity** to avoid washed-out scenes.

- Use **Light Shaft Bloom** on directional lights for cinematic sunlight.

- For night scenes, lower skylight intensity and use **Exponential Height Fog** with colored point lights.

Lumen requires **hardware ray tracing** or **software tracing fallback**. Ensure it's enabled in project settings:

- Project Settings → Rendering → Dynamic Global Illumination: Lumen

- Use **Lumen Reflections** instead of screen-space to support glossy surfaces and complex geometry.

Test your scene under varying time-of-day conditions. Dynamic lighting brings environments to life, but only when balanced. Use **auto exposure settings** sparingly—manual exposure control often yields better artistic direction.

5.3 Nanite Optimization and High-Poly Asset Use

Nanite is Unreal Engine's virtualized geometry system, designed for rendering **billions of triangles** efficiently. It lets you import film-quality assets without compromising performance, dramatically changing how developers approach asset creation.

To use Nanite:

- Enable it on supported static meshes in the mesh editor.

- Use high-detail models (ZBrush sculpts, Quixel Megascans) directly.

- Avoid objects that require vertex animation, like foliage or skinned meshes.

Benefits:

- No need for manual LOD creation.

- Consistent shading across distances.

- Zero pop-in or LOD snapping artifacts.

Nanite excels in environments with:

- Rock formations

- Architectural detail

- Statues, ruins, hard surfaces

For movable objects or foliage, continue using standard meshes with LODs. Avoid Nanite for translucent materials, animated meshes, and objects requiring dynamic tessellation or deformation.

Pair Nanite with **World Partition** to stream parts of large levels only when visible. This creates seamless open-world experiences without sacrificing memory or frame rate.

In short, Nanite allows you to prioritize **artistic fidelity over triangle budgets**, unlocking truly cinematic worlds.

5.4 Material Creation with C++ Control

While many materials in Unreal are built in the Material Editor, there are times when you need to control them programmatically. C++ allows you to dynamically create, apply, or modify materials at runtime based on gameplay logic.

Use the UMaterialInstanceDynamic class to modify material parameters in-game:

cpp

CopyEdit

```cpp
UMaterialInstanceDynamic* DynMaterial =
UMaterialInstanceDynamic::Create(BaseMaterial, this);

Mesh->SetMaterial(0, DynMaterial);

DynMaterial->SetVectorParameterValue("EmissiveColor", FLinearColor::Red);
```

This is especially useful for:

- Changing damage states (e.g., glowing when hit)

- Showing power-ups with material shifts

- Customizing cosmetics or skins

- Applying decals or UI-like materials in the 3D world

To organize materials:

41

- Create **Material Parameter Collections** for global values (e.g., time of day, environment colors).

- Use **Runtime Virtual Textures** to allow world-projected decals that blend with terrain.

Material expressions can also be controlled through Blueprint, but C++ is more efficient when performance or scalability matters. You can batch material updates during state transitions, or optimize updates using tick timers or events.

5.5 Creating Weather Systems with Blueprints + C++

Weather plays a critical role in game atmosphere. Unreal allows you to blend procedural visual effects with gameplay systems to simulate rain, fog, wind, and lightning.

A weather system generally includes:

- **Particle FX** (rain/snow)

- **Audio FX** (ambient sounds)

- **Post-process volumes** (fog, color grading)

- **Lighting manipulation**

- **Gameplay triggers** (e.g., slippery ground)

Use a AWeatherManager actor or component in C++ to manage global weather states. Use enums like EWeatherState::Clear, Rain, Snow, and transition between them over time:

42

cpp

CopyEdit

```cpp
void AWeatherManager::SetWeather(EWeatherState NewWeather)
{
    CurrentState = NewWeather;

    switch (CurrentState)
    {
        case EWeatherState::Rain:
            RainFX->Activate();
            AudioComponent->SetSound(RainSound);
            break;
        // Add other weather types
    }
}
```

Blueprints can hook into this system to control **particle activation, sky color,** or **fog density**. Use timelines to animate smooth weather transitions.

For advanced realism:

- Add wind direction and force.

- Combine cloud movement with weather.

- Trigger puddle materials or wet shaders after rain.

By combining **visual feedback**, **auditory cues**, and **gameplay implications**, weather systems enrich immersion and storytelling.

5.6 Post-Processing for Cinematic Feel

Post-processing is the final polish layer for any visually compelling game. It shapes how scenes feel—whether gritty and tense, dreamy and surreal, or warm and inviting.

Use a **PostProcessVolume** in your scene to apply effects such as:

- **Color grading**

- **Bloom**

- **Ambient occlusion**

- **Vignette**

- **Chromatic aberration**

- **Depth of field**

Set your post-process volume to **Infinite Extent (Unbound)** if you want it to affect the entire world.

C++ can control post-processing dynamically for effects like:

- Player death (fade to black)

- Health-critical state (desaturation)

- Slow motion sequences (DOF blur, motion blur)

Example:

cpp

CopyEdit

```
PostProcessVolume->Settings.bOverride_BloomIntensity = true;

PostProcessVolume->Settings.BloomIntensity = 3.0f;
```

To achieve AAA-style visuals:

- Use LUTs (Lookup Tables) for color grading.

- Simulate lens effects for film-style authenticity.

- Adjust exposure settings manually rather than relying on auto exposure.

Post-process transitions can be tied to gameplay milestones—entering a dungeon, changing biomes, or approaching a boss.

This is where **gameplay meets cinematography**, and where even a simple game world can begin to feel like a living, breathing narrative space.

With Chapter 5 complete, your environments now match the quality of your core systems. You've sculpted dynamic terrain, implemented lighting that reacts to time and space, optimized visuals using Nanite, added responsive weather effects, and polished it all with professional-grade post-processing.

Chapter 6: Crafting Cinematic Sequences and Cutscenes

6.1 Using Sequencer with C++

Unreal Engine's **Sequencer** is a non-linear animation tool used to craft in-game cinematics and real-time cutscenes. While it's commonly driven through the editor, you can control it programmatically with C++—a powerful feature when building dynamic or context-sensitive sequences.

To use Sequencer in C++:

1. Create a **Level Sequence asset** in the editor.

2. In your actor or controller class, include the required headers:

cpp

CopyEdit

```cpp
#include "LevelSequenceActor.h"

#include "LevelSequencePlayer.h"
```

3. In C++, you load and play sequences like this:
   cpp

CopyEdit

```cpp
ALevelSequenceActor* OutActor;
```

```cpp
ULevelSequencePlayer* SequencePlayer =
ULevelSequencePlayer::CreateLevelSequencePlayer(

    GetWorld(), MySequence, FMovieSceneSequencePlaybackSettings(), OutActor);

SequencePlayer->Play();
```

You can also bind camera cuts, character animations, and material changes in the sequence editor, then trigger them in-game with the logic above. This lets you launch cinematics on demand—from entering a location to finishing a quest—without hand-animating everything in C++.

The real strength of this hybrid system is that it **bridges data and narrative**—you can trigger different versions of a scene based on gameplay variables, while retaining the visual polish of a hand-edited cinematic.

6.2 Scripting Cameras and Camera Cuts

Dynamic camera systems are key to immersive storytelling. Unreal lets you create **cinematic camera actors** that simulate real-world lenses, angles, and effects. These can be scripted via C++ or tied to sequences.

To switch between cameras in-game, use SetViewTargetWithBlend:

cpp

CopyEdit

```cpp
APlayerController* PC = UGameplayStatics::GetPlayerController(this, 0);

PC->SetViewTargetWithBlend(MyCameraActor, 1.5f,
EViewTargetBlendFunction::VTBlend_Cubic);
```

Use this for:

- Camera cuts during conversations

- Slow panning introductions

- Boss battle reveals

- Puzzle overviews

You can place multiple cameras in the level or spawn them during runtime. For advanced behavior:

- Attach cameras to moving actors (drones, vehicles).

- Use SpringArmComponent for smoothed movement.

- Create Blueprint "camera director" actors that switch views based on triggers.

In cutscenes, control camera cuts directly in Sequencer. You can animate Field of View (FOV), depth of field, and lens flares for drama and focus.

Design tip: **Treat cameras like characters**—give them intent, weight, and pacing that aligns with the story. A cutscene with purposefully blocked shots feels more cinematic than one with random camera pans.

6.3 Dialogue Systems with DataTables and UI

A compelling narrative demands structured, flexible dialogue systems. In Unreal, this is often built using a mix of **DataTables**, **UMG widgets**, and **C++-driven state management**.

Start by defining a FDialogueLine struct:

cpp

CopyEdit

```cpp
USTRUCT(BlueprintType)

struct FDialogueLine

{
    GENERATED_BODY()

    UPROPERTY(EditAnywhere, BlueprintReadWrite)
    FText SpeakerName;

    UPROPERTY(EditAnywhere, BlueprintReadWrite)
    FText DialogueText;

    UPROPERTY(EditAnywhere, BlueprintReadWrite)
    UTexture2D* Portrait;
```

};

Then create a **DataTable** asset based on this struct. Each row represents a line of dialogue and can be keyed to events, quests, or world state.

In your dialogue manager C++ class:

- Load the table with FindRow.

- Create a function to step through lines.

- Notify the UI with the latest speaker and line.

Build a UMG widget with text blocks and portrait images. Connect them to your logic via BlueprintImplementableEvent or direct function calls.

To display dialogue:

- Pause player input.

- Show the widget.

- Advance on key press or automatically with timers.

For branching dialogue, add options via an array of FText responses and use delegates or callbacks to handle player selection.

Dialogue is more than text—it's rhythm, performance, and timing. Use **animation on widget entries**, camera cuts to show speaker reactions, and voiceover integration if available.

51

6.4 Environmental Storytelling with Volumes and Events

Sometimes the most powerful storytelling happens without words. **Environmental storytelling** uses the game world itself—objects, lighting, placement, sound—to suggest events, emotions, or history.

Unreal offers tools to build these systems organically:

- **Trigger Volumes**: Detect player entry into story-rich areas.

- **Decals**: Blood stains, cracked walls, graffiti—clues embedded in texture.

- **Ambient Sounds**: Play eerie hums or distant cries near mysterious landmarks.

- **Interactive Props**: Let players inspect notes, journals, or old photos.

- **World Building**: Broken toys in a house, candles by a grave, scorched furniture—all narrative clues.

Use OnActorBeginOverlap in C++ to trigger sound, visual effects, or story flags:

cpp

CopyEdit

```
void AStoryVolume::NotifyActorBeginOverlap(AActor* OtherActor)
{
    if (Cast<APlayerCharacter>(OtherActor))
    {
```

```
AudioComponent->Play();

TriggerCinematicEvent();

    }

}
```

Pair this with a persistent quest or story state system to remember player discoveries and evolve the world over time. When done right, players piece together the narrative from fragments, leading to more personal investment and exploration.

6.5 Trigger-Based Cinematics and Conditions

Not all cutscenes should play on a schedule—many are **contextual and reactive**. For that, Unreal's trigger system combined with condition logic in C++ provides an elegant solution.

To implement a conditional cutscene:

1. Place a Box Trigger or custom ACinematicTrigger actor in the level.

2. In the overlap event, check your conditions:

    o   Player has a specific item?

    o   Quest state == Complete?

    o   Enemy defeated?

3. If all conditions are true, play the Level Sequence or camera blend.

Example:

cpp

CopyEdit

```
if (bHasKey && !bCinematicPlayed)
{
    SequencePlayer->Play();
    bCinematicPlayed = true;
}
```

Keep these triggers modular by exposing Conditions as Blueprint-accessible Booleans or enums. That way, level designers can configure when and how a cinematic activates.

You can extend this with:

- **Multiple triggers** for chained scenes

- **Timeline fades** for transitions

- **Actor animations** synced with cinematics

This system ensures that cinematics feel **earned**, not forced—rewarding exploration, puzzle-solving, or completion.

6.6 Reusable Scene Templates for Storytelling

Large games often feature many scenes: dialogue exchanges, flashbacks, puzzle intros. Rather than recreating sequences from scratch each time, build **scene templates**—reusable sequences that adapt based on data.

Structure these templates as Blueprint Actors or Sequence Assets with parameters:

- Camera start/end locations

- Speaker IDs

- Dialogue DataTable row names

- Animation references

In C++ or Blueprint:

- Load the sequence.

- Dynamically bind actor references.

- Feed the correct data into the template.

Example: a conversation system where the camera, characters, and dialogue lines change, but the sequence logic remains identical.

To increase scalability:

- Build a SceneDirectorComponent that handles loading, playing, and restoring game state.

- Separate **scene data** from **scene logic** to avoid rework.

This empowers your team to produce dozens of high-quality cutscenes with minimal extra code—ideal for RPGs, adventure games, or narrative-driven titles.

Chapter 6 transforms your game from a mechanical system into a narrative experience. You've now learned how to direct in-engine cinematics, trigger camera-driven drama, and craft emotionally resonant moments—whether through cutscenes, environmental cues, or branching dialogue.

Chapter 7: Developing Game UI and HUD Systems

7.1 Introduction to UMG and Widgets

In modern game development, the **User Interface (UI)** is more than an overlay—it's an extension of the game world, delivering information, emotion, and interaction. Unreal Engine's UI framework, **Unreal Motion Graphics (UMG)**, empowers developers to build rich interfaces that are visually dynamic and deeply integrated into gameplay.

UMG uses **Widgets**—visual building blocks like images, buttons, progress bars, and text—to construct user interfaces. These widgets are composed using the **Widget Blueprint Editor** or generated and controlled directly from C++.

At the core of UMG is the UUserWidget class, which acts as the container for your UI. You can extend this in C++ to implement logic, bind data, or expose functions to Blueprints. Once created, these widgets are added to the **Viewport** using the player's controller or HUD class:

cpp

CopyEdit

```
UUserWidget* HUDWidget = CreateWidget<UUserWidget>(GetWorld(), HUDClass);

HUDWidget->AddToViewport();
```

UMG supports:

- Fullscreen UI (HUD, menus, pause screens)

- In-world UI (3D widgets on actors or environments)

- Interactive menus and dialogues

- Multi-platform input support (mouse, keyboard, gamepad, touch)

Whether you're building minimal combat HUDs or ornate RPG inventory panels, UMG provides the flexibility to tailor your visual design and functional needs.

7.2 Creating Health Bars, Menus, and Dialogue Boxes

Let's break down three essential UI elements that most games rely on: **Health Bars**, **Menus**, and **Dialogue Boxes**.

Health Bars

Start by creating a new Widget Blueprint (e.g., WBP_HealthBar). Inside:

- Add a ProgressBar widget for visualizing health.

- Bind its value to a float between 0.0 and 1.0.

In your custom C++ character class:

- Create a Health variable and expose it to Blueprints.

- Update the widget via a SetHealthPercentage() method or data binding.

cpp

CopyEdit

```cpp
void UHealthBarWidget::SetHealthPercentage(float Percent)
{
    HealthProgressBar->SetPercent(Percent);
}
```

This allows the widget to respond dynamically to damage or healing events.

Menus

Menus (main menu, pause menu, settings) often require buttons, sliders, and toggles. Structure them into vertical layouts using VerticalBox widgets and bind their events in the Graph tab or via C++.

Menus can pause the game, load levels, or change settings using OnClicked delegates:

cpp

CopyEdit

```cpp
ButtonStart->OnClicked.AddDynamic(this, &UMainMenu::StartGame);
```

59

Dialogue Boxes

Use a TextBlock for speaker name and dialogue content. Display portraits with Image widgets. Store lines in DataTables, as described in Chapter 6, and update text dynamically as players progress through conversations.

Each widget should have a **clean design, intuitive layout, and game-style consistency**—ensuring your UI blends with the aesthetic and tone of your world.

7.3 Binding Data with C++ to Widgets

Dynamic UI requires **real-time data binding** between game logic and UI elements. In Unreal, you bind data in two primary ways:

Direct C++ Updates

Create a reference to the widget and call its exposed methods:

cpp

CopyEdit

```
MyHUD->UpdateAmmo(AmmoCount);

MyHUD->SetObjectiveText(FText::FromString("Find the Key"));
```

This method is explicit, offering tight control and performance.

Bindings in UMG Designer

Widgets can bind to properties using the Bind feature in the UMG editor. You expose properties in your UUserWidget class like so:

cpp

CopyEdit

UPROPERTY(BlueprintReadOnly, Category="UI")

FText CurrentObjective;

Then in Blueprints, use a **Binding Function** to return this value. Be cautious: overly complex bindings evaluated every frame can degrade performance. When possible, update the property only when it changes.

You can also use **Event Dispatchers** to trigger UI updates when game state changes. For instance, when the player picks up an item, broadcast an OnInventoryChanged event to refresh the inventory panel.

This decoupled approach lets you keep UI logic clean and separate from gameplay systems, resulting in code that's easier to maintain and extend.

7.4 Responsive UI for PC, Console, and Mobile

Building UI that works across different platforms and screen sizes requires adaptability. Unreal offers tools to ensure your interface remains legible, usable, and polished across PC monitors, TVs, and mobile screens.

DPI Scaling

Unreal automatically applies **DPI scaling** using its **UI Scale Curve**, which adjusts UI size based on screen resolution. You can modify this curve in **Project Settings → User Interface → DPI Scaling**.

Anchors and Layouts

In UMG:

- Use **Anchors** to position widgets relative to the screen (e.g., top-left, center).

- Use **Canvas Panels**, **Size Boxes**, and **Horizontal/Vertical Boxes** for flexible layout design.

- Use SizeToContent or percentage-based sizing for adaptive design.

Input Handling

Use the **Input Mode Settings** in your PlayerController to handle different input types:

cpp

CopyEdit

```
FInputModeGameAndUI InputMode;

InputMode.SetWidgetToFocus(HUDWidget->TakeWidget());

PC->SetInputMode(InputMode);
```

Support mouse, keyboard, and gamepad with clear visual cues for each (e.g., change prompt from "Press E" to "Press X" on controller). For mobile, ensure buttons are large enough to tap and consider touch-friendly navigation patterns.

Performance Tips for Mobile

- Avoid complex UMG animations with multiple opacity layers.

- Minimize overdraw by using opaque backgrounds and flattening nested widgets.

- Profile UI rendering using the **Unreal Insights** tool.

A responsive interface doesn't just work on every device—it feels **tailored** to that device, respecting user expectations and screen ergonomics.

7.5 Creating Radial Menus and Inventory Systems

Radial menus and **inventory UIs** are often used in games for equipment, skills, or quick actions. These interfaces present unique layout challenges, which UMG can handle with custom logic and geometry.

Radial Menus

To create a radial menu:

- Use Canvas Panel to manually place buttons in circular layout.

- Calculate angles per entry and position buttons using trigonometry in C++ or Blueprint.

cpp

CopyEdit

```
float Angle = (360 / MenuItems.Num()) * Index;

FVector2D Position = Center + Radius * FVector2D(FMath::Cos(Angle),
FMath::Sin(Angle));
```

You can highlight entries based on cursor angle, and confirm selection with input events. Add hover effects and sound feedback for interactivity.

Inventory Systems

Build an UInventoryWidget that displays items using:

- A **Grid Panel** for layout

- A **ScrollBox** for overflow

- UInventoryItemWidget for each slot

Each slot can:

- Show icon and quantity

- Handle clicks or drags

- Highlight on hover or selection

Inventory data is stored in a TArray or TMap on the player character or controller. When items are added or removed, trigger a refresh:

cpp

CopyEdit

```
InventoryWidget->RefreshInventory(PlayerInventory);
```

Add filtering by category, sorting, and tooltips for item details. Tie inventory changes to events like pickups or trades, and update UI accordingly.

Inventory and radial menus add **depth and utility** to your UI, especially when tied to real-time decisions or resource management.

7.6 Polishing with Animations and Sounds

Polished UI feels alive. Small transitions, fade-ins, sounds, and feedback elements dramatically enhance user experience. Unreal's UMG system supports:

Widget Animations

In the UMG editor, create animations by:

- Selecting a widget

- Adding keyframes to the timeline (opacity, scale, position)

- Naming the animation and using PlayAnimation in C++

cpp

CopyEdit

PlayAnimation(MyFadeInAnim);

Use animations for:

- Menu transitions

- Button presses

- Health damage feedback (flashing red overlay)

Sound Cues

Add sound cues to button clicks, hovers, and transitions. Use UAudioComponent for 3D spatial UI (e.g., diegetic menus) or UGameplayStatics::PlaySound2D for traditional flat UI.

For tactile feedback:

- Pair sounds with subtle scale animations on input.

- Use vibration on supported platforms for confirmation cues.

Design your UI polish pass like a cinematographer:

- Guide the eye with motion.

- Reinforce actions with sound.

- Balance clarity with artistry.

When done well, players may not even notice these touches—but they will **feel** them.

With Chapter 7 complete, your game is no longer just playable—it's **presentable**. You now have the tools to build immersive, responsive, and beautiful interfaces that enhance gameplay without distraction. Your UI can now tell stories, convey emotion, and give players seamless control.

Chapter 8: Artificial Intelligence Programming

8.1 AI Controllers, Perception, and Navigation

Artificial Intelligence in Unreal Engine is powered by a layered system of **AI Controllers**, **Perception Components**, and **Navigation Meshes**. These components allow non-player characters (NPCs) to observe, decide, and act in a realistic manner.

An **AI Controller** (AAIController) is a specialized subclass of AController, designed to control pawns through logic rather than player input. It is where behavior trees are initialized, blackboards are assigned, and perception systems are processed.

To begin, create a custom AI controller:

cpp

CopyEdit

```
class AEnemyAIController : public AAIController
{
    GENERATED_BODY()

protected:
    virtual void BeginPlay() override;
};
```

In BeginPlay, you typically initialize the behavior tree:

cpp

CopyEdit

```
UseBlackboard(BlackboardAsset, BlackboardComponent);

RunBehaviorTree(BehaviorTreeAsset);
```

Perception is handled via the **AIPerceptionComponent**. Attach this component in your controller's constructor:

cpp

CopyEdit

```
PerceptionComponent =
CreateDefaultSubobject<UAIPerceptionComponent>(TEXT("PerceptionComponent"));
```

You can configure it to use **Sight**, **Hearing**, or **Damage** senses. For sight:

cpp

CopyEdit

```
SightConfig =
CreateDefaultSubobject<UAISenseConfig_Sight>(TEXT("SightConfig"));

SightConfig->SightRadius = 2000.f;
```

69

```
SightConfig->LoseSightRadius = 2500.f;

SightConfig->PeripheralVisionAngleDegrees = 90.f;

PerceptionComponent->ConfigureSense(*SightConfig);
```

AI needs a **Navigation Mesh (NavMesh)** to move. Place a NavMeshBoundsVolume in
your level and scale it to cover your playable area. Rebuild paths via the Build menu.
Your AI characters must inherit from APawn or ACharacter and use
UNavigationSystemV1::SimpleMoveToActor() or MoveTo() calls in behavior trees.

Together, the AI controller, perception, and navigation systems allow your AI to "see,"
"hear," and move like autonomous agents—reacting intelligently to their surroundings.

8.2 Blackboards and Behavior Trees with C++

Unreal Engine's **Behavior Tree** system provides a modular, visual way to implement AI
logic. It works alongside a **Blackboard**, a data container used to store and access
information relevant to AI decisions.

Creating Behavior Trees and Blackboards

- Create a new **Behavior Tree** and associated **Blackboard** asset in the editor.

- Assign the Blackboard to the AI Controller.

- Use Blackboard Keys like TargetActor, IsAlert, or PatrolIndex to store runtime
  data.

Running from C++

In your AI controller:

cpp

CopyEdit

```
RunBehaviorTree(MyBehaviorTree);

UseBlackboard(MyBlackboard, BlackboardComponent);
```

From here, you can set or get blackboard values in C++:

cpp

CopyEdit

```
BlackboardComponent->SetValueAsObject("TargetActor", DetectedPlayer);
```

Behavior Trees execute tasks in sequence or selectively. Nodes include:

- **Selectors**: Try children until one succeeds.

- **Sequences**: All children must succeed in order.

- **Tasks**: Custom actions like "Move To", "Play Animation".

- **Services**: Run periodically to update blackboard values.

- **Decorators**: Conditional gates that control task execution.

To write a custom behavior tree task:

cpp

CopyEdit

```
class UBTTask_AttackPlayer : public UBTTaskNode
{
    GENERATED_BODY()

public:
    virtual EBTNodeResult::Type ExecuteTask(UBehaviorTreeComponent&
OwnerComp, uint8* NodeMemory) override;
};
```

Return EBTNodeResult::Succeeded, Failed, or InProgress based on task outcome.

With this structure, you can build flexible decision-making processes that adapt to changes in perception, state, and gameplay context.

8.3 Building Patrol, Chase, and Attack Behaviors

Most enemy AI in action or stealth games cycle through three states: **Patrol**, **Chase**, and **Attack**. Unreal's systems allow these to be cleanly implemented using behavior tree tasks and services.

Patrol Behavior

- Store a list of patrol points in your AI pawn.

- On BeginPlay, populate an array or assign index to the blackboard.

- Use a **Move To** task to navigate.

- Create a **Service** that updates the next patrol index when a location is reached.

Chase Behavior

- Triggered by sight or sound.

- Blackboard key TargetActor is set when the player is seen.

- Use Move To task toward TargetActor.

- Add a decorator to only run when TargetActor is not null.

- Use Service to check visibility. If the target is lost for X seconds, revert to patrol.

Attack Behavior

- Engage once in melee or ranged range.

- Stop movement.

- Play an animation or shoot projectile via a custom task.

- Use cooldown timers in blackboard keys to throttle attacks.

Designing these behaviors in a behavior tree ensures readability and modularity. You can inject new conditions, add variants (e.g., flanking, retreating), or create new enemy types with altered trees.

8.4 Environmental Queries (EQS)

The **Environmental Query System (EQS)** allows AI to dynamically evaluate the game world to make smarter decisions—such as finding cover, selecting a target, or identifying the safest path.

EQS is a **data-driven querying system**. Think of it as AI asking: "What's the best location that meets these criteria?"

Enabling EQS

- Enable the **Environment Query System** in Project Settings.

- Create a new **EQ System Query** in the content browser.

Query Example: Find Nearest Cover

1. Add a Generate Points query around the AI.

2. Add Trace tests to check for line-of-sight from enemy.

3. Score points based on distance to player and LOS.

From C++, run EQS with:

cpp

CopyEdit

```cpp
UEnvQueryInstanceBlueprintWrapper* QueryInstance =
UEnvQueryManager::RunEQSQuery(

    this, EQSAsset, this, EEnvQueryRunMode::SingleResult, nullptr);
```

Bind to the query result delegate to respond when a location is found:

cpp

CopyEdit

```cpp
QueryInstance->GetOnQueryFinishedEvent().AddDynamic(this,
&AMyAIController::OnQueryComplete);
```

This allows AI to adapt to terrain, positioning, or group tactics without predefining every possible outcome.

8.5 Dynamic Difficulty via AI Awareness

A smart AI doesn't need to be overwhelming—it needs to feel **responsive**. One way to create this effect is to scale AI difficulty dynamically using **awareness levels** or player behavior tracking.

Awareness System

- Use a float AwarenessLevel (0.0 to 1.0).

- Increase when player is seen, heard, or close.

- Decrease when hidden or distant.

- Tie behavior tree branches to awareness thresholds.

Example:

- Awareness < 0.3: **Patrol**

- Awareness >= 0.3 && < 0.7: **Cautious Search**

- Awareness >= 0.7: **Full Combat**

Player Behavior Metrics

Track how the player behaves:

- Frequency of noise (gunshots, footsteps)

- Visibility time (how long they've been in sight)

- Stealth success/failures

Adjust AI aggression or spawn types accordingly. You can even use these metrics for **adaptive enemy spawning**—fewer enemies if the player is struggling, more if they're breezing through.

Dynamic difficulty creates a game that adapts to skill level without sliders—improving accessibility and immersion simultaneously.

8.6 Optimizing AI Performance in Large Worlds

AI logic can be costly, especially when simulating dozens or hundreds of actors. Unreal provides several optimization strategies:

Use AI LODs

- Implement your own **AI Level of Detail** system:

    - **LOD 0**: Full behavior, animation, and perception

    - **LOD 1**: Limited perception, fewer updates

    - **LOD 2**: Idle state or deactivated

Determine LOD by distance from player or screen visibility. Update only necessary logic on lower LODs.

Limit Ticking

- Avoid enabling bCanEverTick unless absolutely needed.

- Use timers or event-driven systems for infrequent updates.

Use Navmesh Streaming

- For open-world games, divide the world into streaming levels with separate NavMesh volumes.

- Only load and update navigation in active regions.

Behavior Tree Efficiency

- Avoid deeply nested trees or frequent state changes.

- Limit service update intervals (e.g., update every 1s instead of 0.1s).

Blueprint vs C++

- Move frequent AI calculations into C++ where performance is tighter.

- Keep Blueprint logic lightweight and for non-critical behaviors.

Optimizing AI isn't just about CPU savings—it's about **preserving immersion** at scale without sacrificing responsiveness or intelligence.

With Chapter 8 complete, you now possess the knowledge to design and implement AI that behaves convincingly—seeing, reacting, adapting, and performing in line with your game's tone and difficulty. From simple patrol bots to tactical enemies and dynamic challenges, your AI will now stand as a pillar of gameplay design.

Chapter 9: Physics, Interaction, and VFX Systems

9.1 Working with Chaos Physics Engine

Unreal Engine's **Chaos Physics Engine** powers the physical simulation of real-time objects—from falling debris to cloth movement, and destruction sequences. Chaos replaces the older PhysX system and offers a more extensible, performant, and data-driven physics pipeline.

To use Chaos effectively in your game:

- Ensure Chaos Physics is enabled in **Project Settings → Physics → Default Physics Engine**.

- Configure physics settings per actor with Simulate Physics, Enable Gravity, and **Collision Presets**.

Chaos supports:

- **Rigid Body simulation** (falling objects, thrown items)

- **Cloth simulation** (capes, flags)

- **Vehicles** (wheel physics, traction)

- **Field System** (radial force effects, strain fields)

In C++, you can apply forces and impulses dynamically:

cpp

CopyEdit

```
MeshComponent->AddForce(FVector(0.f, 0.f, 50000.f));

MeshComponent->AddImpulse(FVector(1000.f, 0.f, 0.f), NAME_None, true);
```

You can also simulate physical constraints like hinges, springs, and motors using PhysicsConstraintComponent, enabling dynamic behaviors like swinging doors or destructible bridges.

Chaos is GPU-accelerated and deeply optimized—but it demands **collision discipline**. Set proper **mass, damping, and restitution values** to ensure objects interact believably.

For high-fidelity action games or environmental storytelling, Chaos transforms static levels into living, breathing simulations.

9.2 Collision Detection and Hit Events

Collision is foundational to interaction in any 3D game. In Unreal, every actor has one or more **collision shapes**—spheres, capsules, boxes, or custom meshes—defined by **collision presets** and channels.

Each actor's components define:

- **Collision Enabled (NoCollision, QueryOnly, PhysicsOnly, CollisionEnabled)**

- **Collision Response (Block, Overlap, Ignore)**

- **Object Type (Pawn, WorldDynamic, WorldStatic, etc.)**

C++ Example: Detecting a hit on a static mesh actor

cpp

CopyEdit

```
MyMesh->OnComponentHit.AddDynamic(this, &AMyActor::OnHit);
```

Define the hit logic:

cpp

CopyEdit

```
void AMyActor::OnHit(UPrimitiveComponent* HitComponent, AActor* OtherActor,
    UPrimitiveComponent* OtherComp, FVector NormalImpulse, const FHitResult&
Hit)
{
    // Trigger effects, apply damage, or play audio
}
```

Overlap Events are used for non-blocking interactions like pickups or triggers:

cpp

CopyEdit

81

```cpp
TriggerVolume->OnComponentBeginOverlap.AddDynamic(this,
&AMyActor::OnOverlapBegin);
```

To trace for collisions manually, use raycasts or shape traces:

cpp

CopyEdit

```cpp
FHitResult Hit;

FVector Start = GetActorLocation();

FVector End = Start + GetActorForwardVector() * 500;


GetWorld()->LineTraceSingleByChannel(Hit, Start, End, ECC_Visibility);
```

Proper collision setup is vital. Misconfigured presets often lead to frustrating bugs—ensure each component is using the correct channels and responses.

9.3 Building an Object Interaction System

Interactivity adds meaning to the world. Whether you're picking up a torch, pulling a lever, or reading a note, a flexible interaction system connects player agency with game response.

Step 1: Define an Interface

Use a UInterface to establish a consistent interaction contract.

cpp

CopyEdit

```cpp
UINTERFACE(MinimalAPI)

class UInteractable : public UInterface {};


class IInteractable

{

    GENERATED_BODY()


public:

    UFUNCTION(BlueprintNativeEvent, BlueprintCallable)

    void Interact(AActor* Interactor);

};
```

Step 2: Implement the Interface

Apply it to any object (e.g., a door or item) and implement Interact():

cpp

CopyEdit

```cpp
void ADoor::Interact_Implementation(AActor* Interactor)
```

83

```
{

    ToggleOpenState();

}
```

Step 3: Call from the Player

In the player character class, perform a short raycast on input:

cpp

CopyEdit

```
FHitResult Hit;

FVector Start = Camera->GetComponentLocation();

FVector End = Start + Camera->GetForwardVector() * 200.f;


if (GetWorld()->LineTraceSingleByChannel(Hit, Start, End, ECC_Visibility))

{

    if (Hit.GetActor()->Implements<UInteractable>())

    {

        IInteractable::Execute_Interact(Hit.GetActor(), this);

    }

}
```

84

This system is scalable, allowing for hundreds of interactable types without needing tightly coupled logic. Extend it with icons, prompts, or UI feedback via C++ or UMG.

9.4 Reactive Particle FX with Niagara + C++

Niagara is Unreal's advanced **visual effects system**, replacing the older Cascade system. It's modular, GPU-accelerated, and designed for real-time control via C++ or Blueprints.

Step 1: Create a Niagara System

- Use the **Niagara System** wizard.

- Choose an emitter template (e.g., explosion, sparks, smoke).

- Customize behaviors like velocity, color, spawn rate, and life span.

Step 2: Spawn from C++

Include Niagara headers:

cpp

CopyEdit

```
#include "NiagaraFunctionLibrary.h"
```

Spawn effect at a location:

cpp

CopyEdit

```cpp
UNiagaraFunctionLibrary::SpawnSystemAtLocation(GetWorld(), ExplosionFX,
Hit.Location);
```

You can spawn on hit events, overlaps, or gameplay triggers. Niagara also supports parameterized control:

cpp

CopyEdit

```cpp
UNiagaraComponent* FX = UNiagaraFunctionLibrary::SpawnSystemAtLocation(...);

FX->SetFloatParameter("DamageAmount", 100.f);
```

Step 3: Attach to Actors

Spawn effects on actors for persistent visuals—e.g., engine smoke on a damaged vehicle or glowing aura around a power-up.

Use the AttachToComponent() method with a socket name if needed:

cpp

CopyEdit

```cpp
FX->AttachToComponent(Mesh,
FAttachmentTransformRules::SnapToTargetIncludingScale, "Muzzle");
```

86

Niagara systems can be deeply reactive—responding to physics events, player proximity, and animation state.

9.5 Ragdoll Physics and Bone Control

One of the most satisfying visual effects in any game is **ragdoll physics**—letting character bodies react to force realistically when killed or knocked out.

Enabling Ragdoll

1. Ensure your character mesh has a **Physics Asset** (PhAT) defining the bones and constraints.

2. In C++:

cpp

CopyEdit

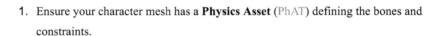

GetMesh()->SetSimulatePhysics(true);

GetMesh()->SetCollisionProfileName("Ragdoll");

This detaches the character from the CharacterMovementComponent, disables input, and lets physics take over.

Apply an impulse to add directionality:

cpp

CopyEdit

```cpp
GetMesh()->AddImpulseAtLocation(ForceVector, HitLocation);
```

Bone Control

For fine-grained control—e.g., head tracking or arm IK—use FABRIK, TwoBoneIK, or LookAt nodes in the Anim Graph. From C++, you can update bone transforms with:

cpp

CopyEdit

```cpp
GetMesh()->SetBoneLocationByName("head", NewLocation,
EBoneSpaces::WorldSpace);
```

This is useful for scripted reactions (e.g., enemies looking toward noise sources) or procedural animation.

Use ragdoll states selectively—often after death, stun, or cinematic moments—then transition back to animation if needed using Blend Physics.

9.6 Destruction and Environmental Effects

Destruction breathes life into static environments. Whether it's a collapsing bridge, a shattering crate, or exploding barrels, **Chaos Destruction** enables real-time breakability.

Step 1: Create a Geometry Collection

- Import a static mesh (e.g., wall).

- Convert it to a **Geometry Collection** using the Chaos plugin.

- Use the Fracture Tool to divide it into clusters (Voronoi, radial, custom).

Step 2: Set Up Destruction Behavior

- Enable simulation and damage thresholds.

- Use field systems (radial force, strain fields) to trigger shattering.

Step 3: Trigger from C++

cpp

CopyEdit

```
ChaosDestructible->ApplyDamage(100.f, ImpactLocation, ImpulseDirection, 500.f);
```

Or use Field System Actors to influence clusters dynamically.

Combine this with Niagara particle effects for dust, debris trails, or fire. Play audio and screen shake for feedback.

Use destructibles sparingly—highly detailed fragments can be expensive on performance. For large-scale destruction (buildings, terrain), break it into multiple chained pieces or use cinematic cut-ins.

Environmental effects can also include:

- **Wind volumes**

- **Volumetric fog** dispersing on entry

- **Cloth reacting to player movement**

- **Lighting flickers during explosions**

These layers make the world **reactive and believable**, creating deeper immersion and emotional engagement.

With Chapter 9 complete, your game now has **reactive physical simulation**, intelligent hit detection, dynamic interactions, and cinematic visual feedback. From high-stakes combat to subtle environmental storytelling, physics and VFX bring your worlds to life—on-screen and in the player's memory.

Chapter 10: Creating an Online Multiplayer Game (Project 2)

10.1 Unreal Networking Basics

Unreal Engine's networking model is built on the **Client-Server architecture**. This means that one instance of the game (the server) holds authority over the world, while all other instances (clients) receive updates and send input to the server.

Understanding key networking roles is crucial:

- **Server**: Owns the authoritative game state. Handles physics, gameplay logic, damage calculation, AI, and game rules.

- **Client**: Responsible for presenting the world to the player. Sends input and receives updates from the server.

- **Listen Server**: A hybrid server-client where the host also plays the game.

- **Dedicated Server**: A headless, non-player instance that only manages game logic and networking.

Unreal handles many low-level tasks—socket communication, packet compression, replication mechanisms—out of the box. However, you must **explicitly control what is replicated** and **which functions are executed where**.

Enable networking in your project by:

- Setting your project's game instance to a custom subclass of `UGameInstance`.

- Configuring multiplayer settings under Project Settings → Maps & Modes.

- Launching multiple PIE (Play In Editor) windows or separate instances for multiplayer testing.

Every multiplayer system in Unreal builds upon the fundamentals of **replication, Remote Procedure Calls (RPCs), and actor ownership**—topics we'll now explore in-depth.

10.2 Replicating Actors and Variables

Replication is the process of syncing data between the server and clients. By default, only actors that explicitly opt in will replicate.

To enable replication on an actor:

cpp

CopyEdit

```cpp
AMyActor::AMyActor()

{

    bReplicates = true;

}
```

Replication can apply to:

- **Actors**: Whole objects like characters, projectiles, or pickups.

- **Variables**: Health, ammo count, position data, or custom states.

To replicate a variable, mark it with UPROPERTY(Replicated) and implement GetLifetimeReplicatedProps:

cpp

CopyEdit

```cpp
UPROPERTY(Replicated)

float Health;


void AMyActor::GetLifetimeReplicatedProps(TArray<
FLifetimeProperty >& OutLifetimeProps) const

{

    Super::GetLifetimeReplicatedProps(OutLifetimeProps);

    DOREPLIFETIME(AMyActor, Health);

}
```

To react when a variable changes, use ReplicatedUsing:

cpp

CopyEdit

```cpp
UPROPERTY(ReplicatedUsing = OnRep_Health)

float Health;


UFUNCTION()

void OnRep_Health()

{

    UpdateHealthBar();

}
```

Only the server can change replicated variables. Clients receive those changes passively. Use server-side functions to modify replicated data in response to client input.

Mastering variable replication allows your players to **see a consistent world**, regardless of location or latency.

10.3 Remote Procedure Calls (RPCs)

RPCs are Unreal's mechanism for sending function calls across the network. Depending on your use case, functions can be marked to execute:

- **Server → Client**

- **Client → Server**

- **Multicast → All Clients**

Server RPC

Executed only on the server, initiated from a client:

cpp

CopyEdit

```
UFUNCTION(Server, Reliable)

void ServerFireWeapon();
```

Client RPC

Executed only on the owning client, typically from the server:

cpp

CopyEdit

```
UFUNCTION(Client, Reliable)

void ClientPlayHitEffect();
```

Multicast RPC

Broadcasts to all clients. Used for global effects like explosions or state changes:

cpp

CopyEdit

```cpp
UFUNCTION(NetMulticast, Reliable)

void MulticastPlayExplosion();
```

Ensure RPCs are called from actors that are **owned** by the caller. The server owns all actors by default; clients can only initiate server RPCs from their `PlayerController` or `PossessedPawn`.

Use `Reliable` when failure is not acceptable (e.g., firing a gun), and `Unreliable` when frequency is high and loss is tolerable (e.g., footstep sounds).

RPCs are your tool for syncing **gameplay intent**—a player fires a weapon, opens a door, or issues a command—and then broadcasting that to the server or peers.

10.4 Syncing Game State Across Clients

In multiplayer games, the **Game State** is the authoritative record of the current match conditions: score, timers, player data, and global game logic.

Use `AGameStateBase` to store replicable information, and `APlayerState` to track per-player data like score, team, or status.

To replicate game-wide variables:

- Use `AGameStateBase`

- Mark variables with `Replicated` and handle logic in `OnRep_` functions.

cpp

CopyEdit

```
UPROPERTY(ReplicatedUsing=OnRep_GamePhase)

EGamePhase CurrentPhase;


void OnRep_GamePhase()

{

    UpdateUI();

}
```

Clients can listen for changes and update HUDs or logic accordingly. For example, when `CurrentPhase` switches to `GameOver`, clients fade the screen and show results.

Each player also has a `PlayerController` and a `PlayerState`. Use `PlayerController` for input and client logic, and `PlayerState` for data like player name, kills, deaths, or achievements.

To keep the world in sync:

- Use replication for data

- Use RPCs for events

- Ensure server validates all client requests

Together, these patterns let players **see the same world, respond to the same rules, and act within a fair system**.

10.5 Lobby, Matchmaking, and Chat Systems

Every multiplayer experience begins in a **lobby**—a place where players gather, choose settings, and prepare for the match. Unreal provides a flexible framework for creating lobbies and managing player transitions.

Creating a Lobby

- Use a custom `GameInstance` to manage persistent data across level loads.

- Host a session using `CreateSession`, and clients join via `FindSessions`.

- Use Blueprint or C++ via `OnlineSubsystem`.

In the lobby level:

- Display a list of connected players using `PlayerState`.

- Assign teams, skins, or loadouts.

- Update lobby UI on player join/leave events.

Matchmaking

For online services (Steam, EOS, custom backends), implement matchmaking via:

- `OnlineSessionInterface`

- Async delegates for `OnFindSessionsComplete`, `OnJoinSessionComplete`

Design your own **ranking or ping filtering logic**, or rely on platform APIs.

Chat System

Use a `Multicast RPC` or a `Server RPC` + `Client RPC` chain:

cpp

CopyEdit

```
UFUNCTION(Server, Reliable)

void ServerSendChatMessage(const FString& Message);


UFUNCTION(Client, Reliable)
```

```
void ClientReceiveChatMessage(const FString& Sender, const
FString& Message);
```

Send messages from the client to the server, validate them, and relay to all clients with sender data.

Add timestamps, mute buttons, and private message functionality as needed. Store chat logs in `TArray<FString>` for scrolling UI.

With these systems, you create a **social framework**—a place where coordination and competition begin long before the match does.

10.6 Testing Multiplayer Sessions and Debugging

Multiplayer development adds complexity. Bugs may only manifest when two clients are out of sync or when replication fails under load. Unreal provides several tools and practices to help test effectively.

Local Testing in Editor

- Use "New Editor Window (PIE)" with multiple players.

- Simulate LAN behavior by choosing **Play As Client/Server**.

- Test authority logic by logging from both ends.

Console Commands

- `net stat net` – View network traffic stats.

- `net pktloss` – Simulate packet loss.

- `net ping` – Force artificial latency.

Network Profiler

Use **Unreal Insights** to trace:

- Replication bandwidth

- RPC frequency

- Net relevancy

This reveals over-replicated data or unoptimized RPC loops.

Common Pitfalls

- Forgetting `bReplicates = true`

- RPCs from non-owned actors

- Over-replicating data each frame

- Missing `DOREPLIFETIME` entries

- Not setting replication conditions

Best Practices

- Minimize replication to only critical data

- Use `COND_SkipOwner` or `COND_OwnerOnly` for targeted updates

- Log authority checks: `HasAuthority()` and `IsLocallyControlled()`

- Always validate client input on the server

Testing is ongoing—each new feature needs multiplayer validation. But once stabilized, your systems will support **real-time, global, cooperative, and competitive gameplay**.

With Chapter 10 complete, you've built the backbone of a multiplayer game—from synchronized player actions and replicated data to lobby systems and matchmaking. You now understand how Unreal Engine's networking systems work at the code level, and how to extend them for real-world production.

Chapter 11: Saving, Loading, and Persistent Worlds

11.1 SaveGame System in C++

Unreal Engine provides a built-in mechanism for saving and loading data via the `USaveGame` system. This system is straightforward, extendable, and works seamlessly with both C++ and Blueprint projects.

To begin, create a subclass of `USaveGame`:

cpp

CopyEdit

```cpp
UCLASS()

class UMySaveGame : public USaveGame

{

    GENERATED_BODY()


public:

    UPROPERTY()

    float PlayerHealth;
```

```
UPROPERTY()

FVector PlayerLocation;


UPROPERTY()

TArray<FString> InventoryItems;
};
```

In your game logic (e.g., PlayerController, GameInstance), create a save instance and store data:

cpp

CopyEdit

```
UMySaveGame* SaveGameInstance =
Cast<UMySaveGame>(UGameplayStatics::CreateSaveGameObject(UM
ySaveGame::StaticClass()));

SaveGameInstance->PlayerHealth = CurrentHealth;

SaveGameInstance->PlayerLocation = GetActorLocation();

UGameplayStatics::SaveGameToSlot(SaveGameInstance,
TEXT("PlayerSaveSlot"), 0);
```

To load data:

cpp

CopyEdit

```cpp
UMySaveGame* LoadedGame =
Cast<UMySaveGame>(UGameplayStatics::LoadGameFromSlot(TEXT("
PlayerSaveSlot"), 0));

if (LoadedGame)
{
    SetActorLocation(LoadedGame->PlayerLocation);

    CurrentHealth = LoadedGame->PlayerHealth;
}
```

This system serializes your data to disk using binary format and is stored in the platform's local save directory. It works out-of-the-box for most needs but can also be extended to support encrypted saves, compression, or cloud storage.

11.2 JSON, Binary, and Cloud Save Options

While USaveGame is powerful, some projects require more control—especially for external storage, analytics, or versioned data. Unreal supports serialization via **JSON, binary**, or integration with **cloud platforms** like Steam or Epic Online Services.

JSON Saving

Use Unreal's `FJsonObject` and `FJsonSerializer` to save data in human-readable form:

cpp

CopyEdit

```cpp
TSharedPtr<FJsonObject> JsonObject = MakeShareable(new FJsonObject());

JsonObject->SetNumberField("Health", PlayerHealth);


FString OutputString;

TSharedRef<TJsonWriter<>> Writer =
TJsonWriterFactory<>::Create(&OutputString);

FJsonSerializer::Serialize(JsonObject.ToSharedRef(),
Writer);


// Save to file

FFileHelper::SaveStringToFile(OutputString, *FilePath);
```

JSON is ideal for debugging, mod support, or syncing structured data with web APIs.

Binary Custom Serialization

For tighter control or optimized file sizes, use `FArchive` for binary read/write:

cpp

CopyEdit

```
FBufferArchive Archive;

Archive << PlayerHealth;

Archive << PlayerLocation;

FFileHelper::SaveArrayToFile(Archive, *FilePath);
```

Unreal's `FMemoryReader` and `FMemoryWriter` allow you to load and write complex structures efficiently.

Cloud Saving

If you're using **Steam**, **Xbox Live**, or **Epic Online Services**, each platform offers cloud syncing. Implement platform-specific APIs or third-party wrappers that abstract slot syncing, conflict resolution, and networked file access.

For example, Steam's `ISteamRemoteStorage` lets you save data directly to the user's cloud profile.

Use `FPlatformFileManager` to detect cloud paths and write your own save-to-cloud wrapper if using a custom backend.

11.3 Autosaving, Checkpoints, and Game Resumes

Modern games often include **autosaving** and **checkpoint** systems to reduce frustration and protect progress.

Autosaving

Set up a **timer** or event-based system in your GameMode or PlayerController:

cpp

CopyEdit

```
GetWorldTimerManager().SetTimer(AutoSaveTimer, this,
&AGameModeBase::Autosave, 60.0f, true);
```

Trigger saves:

- After combat ends

- On entering a safe zone

- After major quest updates

Checkpoints

Define CheckpointActor objects that store save data when the player overlaps:

cpp

CopyEdit

```cpp
void ACheckpoint::NotifyActorBeginOverlap(AActor*
OtherActor)

{

    if (APlayerCharacter* Player =
Cast<APlayerCharacter>(OtherActor))

    {

        SaveCheckpointData(Player);

    }

}
```

Save the checkpoint index, location, and timestamp. When the player dies or loads, they return to the latest checkpoint.

Game Resumes

Detect if a previous save exists on launch, and load it automatically:

cpp

CopyEdit

```cpp
if (UGameplayStatics::DoesSaveGameExist("PlayerSaveSlot",
0))

{
```

```
    LoadGame();

}
```

This allows the player to resume seamlessly after closing the game or a crash—boosting usability and session continuity.

11.4 Player Preferences and Progression

Beyond positional and combat data, many games track **preferences**, **unlockables**, and **meta-progression**.

Store the following in a persistent SaveGame class:

- Audio and video settings

- Keybinds and control layouts

- Completed missions

- Unlocked characters or skins

- XP, level, and achievements

Expose getters and setters in your GameInstance:

cpp

CopyEdit

```
void UMyGameInstance::SetPlayerVolume(float Volume)

{

    PlayerSettings->Volume = Volume;

    SaveGame();

}
```

Apply settings to the engine via UGameUserSettings or by directly modifying runtime components.

Tracking this data across game modes and levels gives players a sense of progression, which increases investment and retention.

Use enums or versioning markers to evolve the save format as features grow.

11.5 Save Slot Management via UI

Players often need to manage **multiple save slots**, each representing a different playthrough or character.

Save Slot Data

Each slot is represented by a named string (SaveSlot_1, SaveSlot_2, etc.) and saved individually.

Create a SaveSlotMetadata struct with:

- Save name

- Timestamp

- Screenshot or thumbnail

- Player level, area, or icon

Save metadata in a persistent index or load it from each file on UI startup.

UI Integration

Build a **Save/Load menu** in UMG with:

- ScrollBox or GridPanel

- Widget for each slot (e.g., `WBP_SaveSlot`)

- Bind slot click to `LoadGameFromSlot()`

Update each slot with:

- Screenshot via `RenderTargetCapture`

- Progress summary

- Last modified time using `IPlatformFile::GetTimeStamp`

Support features like:

- Overwrite confirmation

- Delete slot

- Rename slot

A polished save UI improves trust and gives players control over their game state management.

11.6 Save Compatibility Between Game Versions

As your game evolves, your save files must remain compatible with new data structures and features—especially if you're releasing updates post-launch.

Versioning

Add a SaveVersion property to your SaveGame class:

cpp

CopyEdit

```
UPROPERTY()

int32 SaveVersion = 2;
```

On load, use conditional logic to upgrade or migrate data:

cpp

CopyEdit

```
if (SaveVersion < 2)

{

    UpgradeLegacyFormat(LoadedGame);

}
```

Safe Serialization

Avoid removing or renaming existing UPROPERTY variables. Instead:

- Deprecate them (mark as `meta = (DeprecatedProperty)`).

- Add new variables and initialize them on load.

Custom Load Handling

For breaking changes, consider a **Save Converter Tool** that reads old saves and writes new ones. This is particularly useful in early access titles.

For online games, ensure save data is validated on server-side—reject or patch incompatible formats with migration utilities.

Best Practices

- Backup old saves before testing new builds.

- Always test save/load across version boundaries.

- Keep backward compatibility unless a major release justifies a reset.

Save compatibility ensures trust. When players know their progress is safe, they're far more likely to stick with the game—even through years of updates.

With Chapter 11 complete, your game now has a **persistence layer**—an intelligent system that captures player history, enables choice, and builds continuity. Whether through local autosaves, flexible slot systems, or cloud-synced progression, your players will feel that their investment in your world truly matters.

Chapter 12: Tools Development and Editor Extensions

12.1 Introduction to Slate UI and Editor Scripting

Unreal Engine's editor is built using **Slate**, a powerful C++ UI framework that powers all editor widgets, menus, panels, and custom tools. Alongside Slate is **Editor Utility Widgets** and **Blutility scripting**, enabling developers to add and extend the editor with powerful custom functionality—either visually or through C++.

To begin with custom tool development:

- Add the **EditorScriptingUtilities** and **Slate** modules to your project's `.Build.cs` file.

- Use the **UnrealEd** module to access editor-level commands and extensions.

- Create a new class that inherits from `SCompoundWidget` or `UEditorUtilityWidget`.

Slate is a declarative UI system. For example, a basic button widget in C++ looks like this:

cpp

CopyEdit

```
TSharedRef<SWidget> MyToolUI =
```

```
SNew(SButton)

.Text(FText::FromString("Click Me"))

.OnClicked(FOnClicked::CreateSP(this,
&MyToolClass::HandleClick));
```

Editor scripting allows:

- Batch asset editing

- Custom tool panels

- Level and blueprint automation

- Data validation tools

Slate may have a learning curve due to its verbosity and functional programming style, but it provides **full control over layout, events, and appearance**. If you prefer faster iteration or are working with non-programmers, you can build tools using Editor Utility Widgets (Blueprint-based) and then expand to Slate when needed.

12.2 Creating Custom Level Design Tools

Custom level design tools help designers lay out environments, place assets procedurally, or automate repetitive tasks like setting up volumes or lighting.

Start by creating an **Editor Mode Tool** or **Editor Utility Blueprint**:

- Editor Modes extend the **modes panel**, letting you build tool workflows like painting or placing objects.

- Editor Utility Widgets are faster to set up and ideal for small UI panels.

Example: Mass Placer Tool

Create a panel with:

- Asset picker (for selecting a Static Mesh)

- Numeric input (spawn count, spacing)

- Execute button

In C++ or Blueprint, use the EditorLevelLibrary and EditorAssetLibrary:

cpp

CopyEdit

```
for (int i = 0; i < SpawnCount; i++)

{

    FVector Location = FVector(i * Spacing, 0, 0);

    UEditorLevelLibrary::SpawnActorFromClass(SelectedClass, Location, FRotator::ZeroRotator);

}
```

Other tools might include:

- Snap aligner for props

- Mass collider generator

- Spline-based wall and road generator

- Random foliage populator with density sliders

These tools reduce **design time**, ensure **consistency**, and unlock procedural creativity for world builders.

12.3 Custom Asset Importers with C++

If your game relies on external data—custom file formats, Excel spreadsheets, JSON, or CSV—you can create **Custom Asset Importers** that convert raw data into usable Unreal assets.

To do this, inherit from UFactory:

cpp

CopyEdit

```
UCLASS()

class UCustomDataFactory : public UFactory

{
```

```cpp
GENERATED_BODY()


public:

    UCustomDataFactory();


    virtual UObject* FactoryCreateFile(UClass* InClass,
UObject* InParent,

        FName InName, EObjectFlags Flags, const FString&
Filename,

        const TCHAR* Parms, FFeedbackContext* Warn, bool&
bOutOperationCanceled) override;

};
```

In `FactoryCreateFile`, parse your data and populate a custom UObject or UStruct. Then generate UAssets based on that data—perhaps creating **NPC dialog trees**, **weapon stats**, or **environment descriptors**.

Register the factory with the editor using a module startup class:

cpp

CopyEdit

```
FEditorDelegates::OnAssetPostImport.AddRaw(this,
&FMyModule::HandleImport);
```

Advanced use cases:

- Mass import for localization files

- Syncing assets with a web-based database

- Auto-creating materials from image metadata

This approach **connects Unreal with production pipelines**, minimizing manual setup while maximizing automation.

12.4 Developing Reusable Editor Plugins

Plugins are the most scalable way to build modular, reusable tools for your game—or for distribution across teams or the Unreal Marketplace.

To create a plugin:

- Use the Plugin Wizard in the Editor.

- Choose "Blank Plugin" or "Editor Mode Tool".

- Define module startup/shutdown logic in `MyPluginModule.cpp`.

Each plugin can include:

- Slate-based tool windows

- Custom classes, asset types, factories

- Data processing or pipeline logic

- UI bindings and menu entries

To add a custom toolbar button, use FUICommandList and FExtender:

cpp

CopyEdit

```
FLevelEditorModule& LevelEditor =
FModuleManager::LoadModuleChecked<FLevelEditorModule>("Leve
lEditor");

TSharedPtr<FExtender> Extender = MakeShareable(new
FExtender());

Extender->AddToolBarExtension("Settings",
EExtensionHook::After, CommandList,

    FToolBarExtensionDelegate::CreateRaw(this,
&FMyPlugin::AddToolbarButton));
```

Plugins should:

- Be modular

- Include logging (UE_LOG) and error handling

- Support clean deactivation

- Be tested across engine versions

When built right, editor plugins supercharge Unreal as a **custom development IDE** for your team, adding bespoke functionality specific to your genre, style, and asset pipeline.

12.5 Automating Level Populating Tasks

Large levels demand hundreds of repetitive placements—lights, doors, collectibles, triggers. Automating these tasks improves speed and accuracy.

Use **Editor Scripts** to:

- Find all actors of a type and adjust properties

- Auto-place lighting or reflection captures at grid points

- Assign tags or metadata based on position or naming

- Generate level streaming volumes programmatically

For example, spawn trigger boxes at all door locations:

cpp

CopyEdit

```
TArray<AActor*> Doors;

UGameplayStatics::GetAllActorsOfClass(GetWorld(),
ADoorActor::StaticClass(), Doors);


for (AActor* Door : Doors)
{
    FVector Location = Door->GetActorLocation();

UEditorLevelLibrary::SpawnActorFromClass(ATriggerBox::Stati
cClass(), Location, FRotator::ZeroRotator);
}
```

You can also:

- Align props to terrain

- Batch name actors

- Auto-create audio zones with falloff curves

Automation frees your level designers from tedium and ensures **visual and functional consistency** across levels.

12.6 Building Tools for Artists and Designers

Great tools aren't just functional—they're **usable, discoverable, and empowering**. When building tools for artists, focus on:

- **Minimalist UI**: Show only what matters. Use collapsible panels, tabs, and context-sensitive displays.

- **Live Preview**: Visual feedback for sliders, toggles, and changes—instant gratification boosts adoption.

- **Error Handling**: Graceful fallbacks, warnings, and sanity checks (e.g., "No asset selected").

- **Customization**: Allow designers to save settings, set favorites, or create presets.

- **Documentation**: Include tooltips, in-editor guides, or even sample usage assets.

Example Tools for Artists:

- **Decal randomizer**: Apply randomized rotation, scale, and material variants to placed decals.

- **Material creator**: Automatically create material instances from texture folders.

- **Prefab painter**: Paint random groups of static meshes onto terrain using a brush system.

You can also integrate feedback from artists directly:

- Build features in response to common friction points.

- Pair program with artists to understand their workflows.

- Collect usage data (e.g., tool opened X times, most used settings).

A well-crafted tool **extends creative freedom**—reducing technical overhead and letting the visual team focus on storytelling and polish.

With Chapter 12 complete, you've crossed into the domain of Unreal Engine power users—building **custom editor interfaces, procedural design tools, asset workflows, and automation systems** that elevate development across your entire team. Your game is no longer just a runtime experience—it's supported by tools that save time, improve quality, and scale production.

Chapter 13: Optimization and Performance Tuning

13.1 Profiling with Unreal Insights

Optimization begins with **profiling**. Guesswork leads to unnecessary rewrites and missed bottlenecks. Unreal Engine's official tool, **Unreal Insights**, provides deep diagnostics across threads, frames, and system events.

What Unreal Insights Tracks:

- Game thread and render thread timing

- Memory allocations

- Garbage collection events

- Asset loading and streaming

- Networking activity

- Custom user events (via trace logging)

Setting Up

1. Enable `UnrealInsights` via the **Session Frontend** or by launching it directly (`UnrealInsights.exe`).

2. Start a profiling session:

   ○ In Editor: `stat startfile`

   ○ Stop capture: `stat stopfile`

   ○ The trace file will be saved to your project folder under `Saved/Profiling`.

3. Open the trace in **Unreal Insights**, and use the Timeline View to identify:

   ○ Long-running tasks on the **Game Thread** (AI, logic)

   ○ **Render Thread** delays (overdraw, shader compilation)

   ○ **Asset loads** or blocking I/O on the main thread

You can create **custom trace events** in C++ using `TRACE_CPUPROFILER_EVENT_SCOPE`:

cpp

CopyEdit

```
TRACE_CPUPROFILER_EVENT_SCOPE(MyFunctionPerformance);
```

Use Insights regularly, especially before optimization passes. Profiling reveals the truth—and lets you fix real problems, not perceived ones.

13.2 FPS Bottlenecks: Draw Calls, Ticks, and GC

Smooth gameplay depends on maintaining frame rate (FPS). Performance drops can originate from the CPU or GPU—or both. Three major culprits are **draw calls, tick functions**, and **garbage collection**.

Draw Calls

Each object that must be rendered with a unique material or state requires a draw call. High draw call counts strain the GPU and render thread.

To reduce draw calls:

- Use **Instanced Static Meshes (ISM)** or **Hierarchical ISMs (HISM)**

- Merge static meshes in the editor or via `Merge Actors` tool

- Minimize material variety and shader complexity

Monitor with `stat rhi` and `stat scenerendering`.

Ticks

Too many tick-enabled actors cause CPU bottlenecks. Each tick function adds overhead per frame.

Reduce tick cost by:

- Disabling `bCanEverTick` unless needed

- Using **timers** or **delegates** for non-per-frame logic

- Grouping similar logic into manager actors

Use `stat game` to monitor tick time and `stat actor` to see tick contributors.

Garbage Collection (GC)

Excessive memory allocations or poorly managed references can spike GC time.

Avoid:

- Creating UObjects in tight loops

- Holding transient data in UPROPERTY references

- Forgetting to `MarkPendingKill()` on deleted actors

Track GC time with `stat memory` and `stat gc`. Clean up memory leaks and reduce short-lived UObject churn.

Together, these factors directly influence **playability, input responsiveness, and visual smoothness**—make them top optimization priorities.

13.3 LODs, Instancing, and Occlusion Culling

Visual fidelity shouldn't come at the cost of performance. Smart use of **Level of Detail (LOD)** systems, instancing, and **occlusion culling** ensures that only what's needed is rendered.

LODs (Level of Detail)

Meshes with LODs reduce triangle counts based on distance.

- Create LODs in modeling software or auto-generate in Unreal.

- Use **Screen Size** thresholds to trigger LOD swaps.

- For skeletal meshes, ensure LODs include reduced bone influence and animation complexity.

Enable `r.ViewMode LODColoration` to visualize active LODs in-game.

Instancing

Replace repeated static mesh actors with **Instanced Static Mesh Components**. This drastically reduces draw calls.

Ideal for:

- Grass, rocks, trees

- Buildings with repeating units

- Modular level kits

Use HISM for hierarchical culling across large scenes.

Occlusion Culling

Unreal's GPU-based occlusion culling skips rendering for fully obscured objects.

- Ensure `Bounds` are accurate and not overly large

- Avoid overly complex transparent materials (they can't be occluded)

- Use `r.HZBOcclusion 1` to enable Hierarchical Z-Buffer (default in UE5)

Visualize culling with `r.visualizeOccludedPrimitives 1`.

These systems make it possible to build expansive, detailed worlds without sacrificing FPS—especially on lower-end systems or consoles.

13.4 Optimizing C++ Code and Garbage Collection

C++ is powerful, but poor coding practices can lead to performance regressions that snowball over time. Proper memory and logic management is critical.

Avoid Heavy Logic in Ticks

Move infrequent logic into event-driven systems. For example, collision checks should trigger on overlap events—not be manually queried every frame.

Use Stack Allocations Where Possible

Instead of using `new` or allocating on the heap:

cpp

CopyEdit

```
FVector TempVec; // Stack allocated
```

This avoids GC overhead and improves cache performance.

UObject Lifecycle

Only allocate UObjects when you need engine-level features like reflection or garbage collection. For logic-only helpers, use regular C++ classes.

Avoid:

cpp

CopyEdit

```
NewObject<UMyTempObject>() // Each one is tracked by GC
```

Use:

cpp

CopyEdit

```
TSharedPtr<FMyStructHelper> TempHelper =
MakeShared<FMyStructHelper>();
```

TArray Pitfalls

Preallocate with Reserve() when possible to avoid resizing overhead. Avoid repeatedly removing elements in loops—use RemoveAtSwap() if order isn't needed.

GC Tips

- Use `TWeakObjectPtr` instead of `UPROPERTY()` when references don't need to be strong.

- Remove unnecessary `UPROPERTY()` annotations from internal variables.

- Avoid circular references (A owns B, B owns A)—this leads to leaks unless explicitly nullified.

With disciplined C++ code, your systems will not only be faster—they'll scale predictably and remain maintainable through development cycles.

13.5 Packaging for Low-End Devices

Optimizing for mobile or low-spec hardware is more than just reducing resolution—it's about **tailoring the experience** and **minimizing overhead**.

Texture and Material Optimization

- Use **compressed formats** (ETC2 for Android, DXT1 for Windows).

- Avoid high-resolution textures where not needed.

- Reduce material complexity (limit layers, refractions, dynamic parameters).

Mesh Optimization

- Use LODs aggressively.

- Limit bone count on characters.

- Merge small meshes where possible.

Platform-Specific Settings

In Project Settings:

- Use different **Scalability settings** for each platform.

- Turn off real-time shadows if GPU-bound.

- Disable motion blur, ambient occlusion, or post-processing effects.

Mobile-Ready Rendering

Switch to **Mobile Renderer** when building for Android or iOS. Use `Forward Shading` with baked lighting to reduce draw costs.

For packaging:

- Choose appropriate APK size targets.

- Use `Pak` file chunking for level streaming or staged updates.

Always test on real devices. Simulators can't replicate real GPU limits, thermal throttling, or memory constraints.

13.6 Console Commands for Debugging

During development, **console commands** provide instant insights and control. Whether you're diagnosing performance or tweaking visual fidelity, these tools are invaluable.

Performance Commands

- `stat unit` – Show Game, Draw, GPU thread times

- `stat fps` – Display FPS

- `stat memory` – Show memory usage

- `stat sceneRendering` – Breakdown of render performance

Rendering and Debugging

- `r.ViewMode LODColoration` – Visualize LODs

- `r.ShadowQuality 0-5` – Toggle shadow detail

- `r.Fog 0/1` – Toggle fog

- `r.Streaming.PoolSize 1500` – Cap texture pool usage

Replication

- `net stat net` – Show network traffic

- `net pktlag=X` – Simulate latency

- `net pktloss=X` – Simulate packet loss

Gameplay

- `pause` – Toggle game pause

- `slomo X` – Slow/speed up time (1.0 is normal)

Use console commands in PIE or packaged builds with developer access enabled. For debugging crashes or spikes, combine `stat commands` with **Unreal Insights** for deeper analysis.

With Chapter 13 complete, you've equipped your game with the tools and practices necessary for **performance parity across platforms**. From frame-level optimizations to memory and packaging strategies, your project is now ready to scale and run smoothly—whether on a desktop powerhouse or a mobile chipset.

Chapter 14: Packaging, Publishing, and Monetizing

14.1 Preparing Your Game for Release

Before shipping your game, it's critical to transition from a development mindset to a **release-ready production process**. This includes stabilization, compliance, optimization, and polishing of core systems.

Here's what must be finalized:

- **Content Lock**: Define a final build cutoff—no new features, only fixes.

- **QA Passes**: Test every system, level, and mechanic with reproducible checklists.

- **Save System Verification**: Ensure backward compatibility and reliability across sessions.

- **Localization & Regional Testing**: Include multiple language support if targeting global markets.

- **Achievements and Analytics**: Integrate tracking via Epic Online Services, Steam, or PlayFab.

- **Build Labels and Versioning**: Implement consistent semantic versioning (v1.0.0), commit tagging, and changelog systems.

Audit your asset pipeline:

- Remove unused assets.

- Compress oversized textures.

- Validate audio cue links, navigation meshes, and broken references.

Final prep includes:

- **Default maps and startup settings** in `Project Settings → Maps & Modes`.

- Ensuring `Shipping` build config has **asserts, debug logs, and developer cheats disabled**.

- Testing in **Standalone** and **Packaged** modes with multiple save paths.

A stable and predictable release build saves your team time, minimizes patching, and builds early trust with your player base.

14.2 Packaging for PC, Console, and Android

Unreal Engine supports a wide range of platforms, each requiring specific packaging setups and configurations.

Packaging for PC (Windows, Linux)

- Go to `File → Package Project → Windows`.

- Use `Shipping` configuration for production builds.

- Enable or disable `Pak` files based on whether you need loose file access or encrypted assets.

- Add `DefaultGame.ini` settings for window resolution, VSync, and user input configs.

- Use launch arguments like `-NoSplash` and `-Fullscreen` as needed.

Packaging for Android

- Install **Android Studio + SDK/NDK**.

- Set paths in `Project Settings → Android SDK`.

- Configure:

  ○ Package name

  ○ API level

  ○ Minimum device specs

  ○ Permissions (camera, storage)

- Choose between **ETC2**, **ASTC**, or **DXT** texture compression formats.

- Enable `armv7` or `arm64` architecture.

Use `gradle` packaging and bundle options (`.apk`, `.aab`) for Google Play submission. Test on multiple Android devices—emulators are insufficient.

Packaging for Console

Console development requires NDA access, dev kits, and platform SDKs (Xbox, PlayStation, Nintendo Switch).

Unreal supports console builds natively once the appropriate **platform plugins and SDKs** are installed. Expect to:

- Handle platform certification requirements (TRCs, LotCheck, TCRs)

- Support platform-specific save APIs

- Integrate achievement/trophy systems

- Adjust input/UI flow to match console UX standards

Packaging console builds is highly regulated. Work closely with the platform partner (Sony, Microsoft, Nintendo) for publishing pipelines.

14.3 Epic Games Store and Steam SDK Integration

Publishing on digital stores requires **SDK integration, backend configuration, and client-side validation**.

Epic Games Store (EGS)

- Use the **Epic Online Services (EOS) SDK** to integrate achievements, leaderboards, matchmaking, and stats.

- Upload builds via the **Dev Portal**.

- Set product pages, pricing, supported platforms, and region restrictions.

- Handle authentication and in-game purchase hooks with EOS interfaces.

Add online subsystem modules:

cpp

CopyEdit

```
OnlineSubsystemEOS

OnlineSubsystem
```

Steam SDK

- Install the **Steamworks SDK**.

- Integrate with `OnlineSubsystemSteam`.

- Add your App ID to `steam_appid.txt`.

142

Key features:

- Steam overlay

- Workshop integration

- Cloud saving

- Achievements and stats

Enable in `DefaultEngine.ini`:

ini

CopyEdit

```
[OnlineSubsystem]

DefaultPlatformService=Steam
```

Use `Steamworks` APIs to manage user sessions, downloadable content (DLC), matchmaking lobbies, and game stats.

Both platforms require you to:

- Submit builds

- Create metadata (images, trailers, tags)

- Pass technical reviews

- Handle payments and region-based pricing

14.4 Creating Installers and Patches

Distributing your game outside of major platforms may require **custom installers, patch systems, or launchers**.

Installers

Use tools like:

- **NSIS** or **Inno Setup** for lightweight Windows installers.

- **Butler** (for Itch.io)

- **InstallShield**, **BitRock**, or **Clickteam** for professional-grade packages.

Include:

- License agreement

- Directory selection

- Shortcut creation

- Optional dependencies (DirectX, Visual C++ redistributables)

Patching Systems

For live service games:

- Use chunk-based patching via Unreal's **Hotfix/ChunkDownloader plugin**.

- Leverage Pak file updates and Manifest files.

- Serve updates over HTTPS/CDN.

For Steam, use **Depot Build Tools** to push patches. For EGS, manage builds via product versioning and branch updates.

Support delta updates to reduce file size. Always checksum files post-download to avoid corrupted installations.

14.5 Monetization: DLC, Cosmetics, and Ads

Revenue generation must be **player-first, fair, and scalable**. Unreal provides systems and patterns for implementing monetization:

DLC (Downloadable Content)

- Package additional content as separate levels, Blueprints, or assets.

- Use Pak files or Steam/EGS DLC mechanisms.

- Gate features or content using HasDLC() checks from platform APIs.

In-Game Store (Cosmetics, Skins, etc.)

- Build a UI to browse purchasable items.

- Use `FString ItemID`, `Price`, `Currency` for each offer.

- For premium items, store purchase data via platform entitlement or server-side APIs.

- Apply cosmetics by changing material instances, meshes, or animation sets.

Ad Integration

For mobile games:

- Use third-party SDKs (AdMob, Unity Ads).

- Trigger ad requests during appropriate moments (e.g., end of match, level complete).

- Respect user experience: avoid spamming or forced viewing.

Monetization should **never hinder gameplay**. The best systems enhance the experience, offer personalization, or extend playtime through meaningful optional content.

14.6 Marketing Strategy and Launch Checklists

No matter how good your game is, it won't sell without **visibility**. Marketing should begin **long before release**, building anticipation and community engagement.

Pre-Launch Strategy

- Create a **Steam page** or **EGS product listing** early.

- Launch a teaser site or dev blog.

- Share consistent content: behind-the-scenes, devlogs, GIFs, polls.

- Build a **press kit** with logos, trailers, and review copies.

Launch Checklist

- ■ Game has no critical bugs, crashes, or save corruption.

- ■ Builds uploaded and approved on distribution platforms.

- ■ Store pages set live with optimized descriptions, tags, and SEO.

- ■ Achievements, cloud saves, and multiplayer features tested.

- ■ Social channels primed (Twitter, Discord, TikTok, Reddit).

- ■ Community moderation and support channels set up.

Post-Launch

- Announce roadmap.

- Track feedback and crash analytics.

- Hotfix within 24–48 hours of launch bugs.

- Engage your audience via community challenges or developer AMAs.

A focused marketing strategy backed by a smooth release pipeline ensures **long-tail success and positive word of mouth**—two pillars of modern indie and AA game launches.

With Chapter 14 complete, your game is now **ready to enter the market**. You've learned how to package it professionally, deploy to major stores, support monetization strategies, and plan a launch that captures attention and builds community.

Chapter 15: Portfolio Projects with Source Code

15.1 Project Overview: Third-Person Action Adventure

This project is a polished third-person action game template—designed to demonstrate a full gameplay loop, camera systems, interaction, combat, and exploration mechanics, all built in **C++ with Blueprint integration**.

Key Features

- Fully controllable third-person player character with animation blueprint

- Sprinting, jumping, climbing, crouching

- Modular combat system (melee and ranged support)

- AI enemy types with patrol, chase, and attack states (BT + C++)

- Inventory and pickup system

- Quest system with objectives and visual prompts

- Interactive environment: switches, levers, destructibles

- Save/load system and main menu with slot management

- Lumen-based dynamic lighting and optimized Nanite environments

Technical Highlights

- Uses Enhanced Input System for fluid player control

- Advanced AI using Blackboard, Behavior Trees, and EQS

- Integrated Niagara particle systems for combat feedback

- Fully documented modular C++ code structure

Showcase Value

- Demonstrates deep gameplay programming skills

- Perfect for technical design, gameplay engineer, or generalist roles

- Clean project folder and class hierarchy—recruiters and leads can navigate easily

15.2 Project Overview: Narrative-Driven Walking Sim

This project is a minimalist, story-first walking simulator designed to showcase **level design, environmental storytelling, dialogue systems**, and world-building techniques.

Key Features

- First-person character with mouse/keyboard or gamepad support

- Spline-guided level progression and auto-save checkpoints

- Dialogue system using DataTables and UMG widgets

- Cinematic sequences triggered via volume or condition

- Dynamic ambient audio with Wwise-style blend zones

- Interaction system for notes, doors, audio logs

- Custom lighting, fog, and post-process for atmosphere control

Technical Highlights

- Uses Sequencer and Level Blueprint for scene scripting

- Editor Utility Widgets for content tagging and metadata

- UI built with C++ logic + Blueprint widgets for dialogue and subtitles

- SaveGame system for narrative branches and progress

Showcase Value

- Ideal for level designers, narrative designers, and cinematic-focused developers

- Highlights world-building and player experience

- Visual polish and ambient tone reflect artistic intent

15.3 Project Overview: Online PvP Shooter (Lite)

This is a **networked multiplayer template** that simulates a simple PvP arena shooter with dedicated server support and online session handling.

Key Features

- Two-player online deathmatch using LAN/Steam

- Shooter mechanics: aim, fire, reload, projectile and hitscan

- Customizable weapons and damage values

- Replicated characters and animations

- Dedicated lobby, match timer, and scoreboard

- Game State and Player State synchronization

- Respawn system and kill feed

- Optional bot support for offline testing

Technical Highlights

- Built on Unreal's native networking model

- Client-server authority logic with full use of RPCs

- Session creation/joining via Online Subsystem

- Optimized replication setup using conditional properties and minimal bandwidth

Showcase Value

- Perfect for gameplay/network programmers

- Demonstrates deep knowledge of online multiplayer in Unreal

- Acts as a standalone showcase or base for competitive game projects

15.4 How to Fork, Modify, and Expand These Projects

Each project is made **open-source and extensible** so you can:

- **Fork on GitHub** for your private repo

- Add your own mechanics, environments, or polish

- Use modular folder structure for easy replacement

Expansion Ideas

- For Action Adventure: Add a boss fight, crafting system, or minimap

- For Walking Sim: Integrate full voiceover, branching endings, or player choices

- For PvP Shooter: Add team modes, leaderboard integration, or new weapon classes

Projects are built with a **component-based architecture**—meaning systems like health, interaction, and movement are self-contained and reusable.

Refactor classes, add Blueprint child classes, or replace assets—this codebase is meant to be **your playground**.

Development Tips

- Use `git checkout -b feature/MyAddition` for new features

- Commit early and often with descriptive messages

- Write changelogs when showcasing work to studios

15.5 GitHub Repo Access and Setup Guide

All projects are available in the companion GitHub repository:

🔗 **github.com/YourUsername/UnrealGameDevProjects**
(Replace with your custom link)

Setup Steps

Clone the repo:

bash
CopyEdit

```
git clone
https://github.com/YourUsername/UnrealGameDevProjects.git
```

1.

2. Run `GenerateProjectFiles.bat`

3. Open the `.uproject` file with Unreal Engine 5+

4. Build from source in Visual Studio or Rider

5. Hit "Play" in the editor or package as needed

All projects follow:

- Clean naming conventions

- Source + Content folder separation

- ReadMe with setup and usage instructions

- Version tags and branches for UE5.0, 5.1, etc.

These are **production-ready base projects**, suitable for real portfolio use, prototyping, or even commercial expansion.

15.6 Using These Projects in a Job Portfolio

A great project isn't just one that runs—it's one that **shows your thinking, your decisions, and your structure.**

Portfolio Best Practices

- Host source code on GitHub with a clear ReadMe

- Include **short gameplay clips** or **feature walkthroughs**

- Use **branching** to show progress or experimental ideas

- Document classes or modules with inline comments

What Recruiters Look For

- Clean code structure (comments, modularity, naming)

- Understanding of Unreal's architecture (replication, components, UCLASS/UPROPERTY)

- Performance and scalability awareness

- Problem-solving evidence (e.g., workaround for known Unreal bug)

How to Present Projects

- Include in personal website or LinkedIn

- Create DevLog posts or YouTube demos

- Highlight individual contributions if on a team

- Prepare to answer: "What would you do differently next time?"

Portfolio projects are not just about what you made—they're about **how you think** and **how you build**. These sample projects offer a polished foundation, but the real value comes from how you shape them into something unique and personal.

With Chapter 15 complete, your journey through Unreal Engine and C++ game development reaches its practical apex. You now have **ready-to-use, production-tier projects** backed by real engine code, replication systems, cinematic features, and responsive UI—all suitable for commercial work or career opportunities.

Appendix A: C++ Quick Reference for Unreal Developers

Keywords, Macros, and Syntax Refreshers

Element	Description
`class`, `struct`	Basic building blocks of C++ objects. In Unreal, use `UCLASS()` and `USTRUCT()` when reflection is needed.
`public`, `private`, `protected`	Access modifiers for members—Unreal relies on `public` for Blueprint exposure.
`virtual`, `override`	Used for inheritance. Unreal methods like `BeginPlay()` or `Tick()` are overridden this way.
`const`, `static`, `inline`	Important for performance and compile-time control.
`#include`	Brings in headers. Avoid including everything—use forward declarations where possible.

| `template,` | Unreal's version of standard containers with reflection support. |
| `TArray, TMap` | |

Header Files, UPROPERTY, UFUNCTION Summary

UPROPERTY Specifiers (Common)

- `VisibleAnywhere`: Viewable in editor, not editable.

- `EditAnywhere`: Editable in editor and defaults.

- `BlueprintReadWrite`: Access from Blueprints.

- `Replicated`: Network sync on variable.

- `Transient`: Not saved or serialized.

UFUNCTION Specifiers (Common)

- `BlueprintCallable`: Usable in Blueprint graphs.

- `Server, Client, NetMulticast`: For RPCs.

- `Exec`: Callable from console commands.

- `Reliable, Unreliable`: For network reliability.

Common Pitfalls and Debugging Tricks

Pitfall	Solution
Forgotten `bReplicates = true`	Always set this in replicated actors.
Crashes from null pointers	Use `IsValid()` or check `nullptr` before accessing.
Tick overload	Replace frequent ticks with `FTimerHandle` or events.
Blueprint not updating	Check for missing `BlueprintCallable`, or hot reload issues.
Asset references failing	Use `TSoftObjectPtr` or `ConstructorHelpers` safely.

Debug Tips

- Use `UE_LOG(LogTemp, Warning, TEXT("Value: %f"), MyVar);`

- Add `ensure()` or `check()` to validate runtime conditions.

- Attach debugger in Visual Studio to track stack traces.

- Use `stat` commands to benchmark runtime costs.

Appendix B: Unreal Engine Cheatsheet

Editor Shortcuts

Action	Shortcut
Play in Editor	`Alt + P`
Focus on Actor	`F`
Translate	`W`
Rotate	`E`
Scale	`R`

Snap to Floor	End
Duplicate	Alt + Drag or Ctrl + W
Content Browser	Ctrl + Shift + F

Blueprint-to-C++ Conversions

Blueprint Node	C++ Equivalent
Delay	FTimerHandle with GetWorldTimerManager()
Print String	UE_LOG()
Branch	if (Condition)
Cast To	Cast<>()

| Spawn Actor | `GetWorld()->SpawnActor<>()` |

Performance Optimization Checklist

- ■ Use Instanced Static Meshes for repeated assets

- ■ Reduce tick usage, use timers instead

- ■ Implement proper LODs for meshes

- ■ Profile using `Unreal Insights`

- ■ Avoid spawning too many dynamic lights

- ■ Use pooled Niagara FX or object pooling

Input Mapping Table

Action	Platform	Input
MoveForward	PC/Console	W / Left Stick Y+
Jump	All	Space / Gamepad A

Fire	PC	Left Mouse
Sprint	Console	L3 Button
Interact	Mobile	UI Button / Screen Tap

Project File Structure Summary

Folder	Purpose
/Source/ProjectName	Main game C++ logic
/Content/Blueprints	Blueprint classes
/Content/Maps	Game levels
/Content/Materials	Master and instance materials

| `/Content/UI` | Widget Blueprints and UI assets |
| `/Config` | INI settings for input, engine, and project |

Appendix C: Asset & Tools Directory

Recommended 3D Model Libraries

- <u>Quixel Megascans</u> – Free for Unreal users, high-quality photogrammetry

- <u>CGTrader</u> – Commercial and free assets

- <u>Sketchfab</u> – Great for prototyping and indie games

- Kenney Assets – Clean, stylized open-source assets

Free and Paid Marketplace Plugins

- **Easy Multi Save** – For advanced SaveGame systems

- **Advanced Sessions** – Better multiplayer session control

- **VaRest** – REST API calls from Blueprints

- **RiderLink / Visual Assist** – Enhanced C++ IDE support

Level Design Templates

- **City Sample** – For urban open-world layouts

- **Shooter Game Template** – Great multiplayer baseline

- **Adventure Kit** – Quest, inventory, and dialogue starter pack

Tools for Sound, Animation, and Storyboarding

- **Audacity** – Free audio editing

- **Reaper** – Affordable DAW for voice processing

- **Mixamo** – Auto-rigging and animation preview

- **Krita / Storyboarder** – Visual planning and animatic tools

GitHub Tools and Scripts Used in the Book

- AutoLOD Setup Scripts

- NavMesh Batch Generation Scripts

- EnhancedInput C++ Mapping Helper

- UnrealPak chunk config templates

- Git pre-commit hook for asset renaming

Appendix D: Developer Career Guide

How to Use This Book to Land a Job

- Use the portfolio projects (Chapter 15) to show **real game-ready systems**.

- Build a **modular, clean GitHub profile** with each project isolated and well-documented.

- Prepare **walkthroughs and screenshots** showing design choices, structure, and gameplay loops.

Building a Public Portfolio Website

- Host with GitHub Pages, Netlify, or WordPress.

- Include:

    ○ Game projects (images + videos)

    ○ Downloadable resume

    ○ About You (your role, tech stack)

    ○ Links to GitHub and LinkedIn

Use tools like **Notion**, **Semplice**, or **Carrd** for quick deployment.

Resume and LinkedIn Tips for Game Developers

Section	What to Include
Summary	2–3 sentences on your specialty (Unreal/C++, gameplay, AI, tools)
Projects	Bullet points showing features you coded, problems solved
Skills	C++, Unreal, Blueprints, Git, Networking, AI, etc.

Experience   Even if it's freelance, modding, or solo—you did the work

On LinkedIn:

- Use cover images showcasing your game

- Write posts about updates, behind-the-scenes

- Join Unreal developer groups and participate

Interview Questions from Real Studios

Category	Example Question
C++	Explain `virtual`, `override`, and object slicing
Unreal	How do you replicate a variable with a custom reaction?
Debugging	How would you find a memory leak in a ticking actor?
Gameplay	How do you make AI choose between melee and ranged attacks?

Prepare mini-projects or whiteboard flows for **systems design**.

Indie Dev: Freelancing and Revenue Models

- Use **Itch.io**, **Epic Store**, **Steam** for solo publishing.

- Monetize via:

    - One-time purchase (premium)

    - Episodic content (DLCs)

    - Cosmetic monetization

    - Patreon or Ko-fi support models

Join communities:

- **Indie Hackers, r/gamedev, Unreal Slackers Discord**

Start small, ship often, and focus on **value per player** rather than features per sprint.

www.ingramcontent.com/pod-product-compliance
Lightning Source LLC
La Vergne TN
LVHW051336050326
832903LV00031B/3571